McWilliams, Dean

John Gardner

John Gardner

Twayne's United States Authors Series

Warren French, Editor

University of Wales, Swansea

TUSAS 561

John Gardner
Photograph © 1989 Nancy Crampton.

John Gardner

By Dean McWilliams

Ohio University

Twayne Publishers • Boston
A Division of G. K. Hall & Co.

John Gardner
Dean McWilliams

Copyright 1990 by G. K. Hall & Co.
All rights reserved.
Published by Twayne Publishers
A Division of G. K. Hall & Co.
70 Lincoln Street
Boston, Massachusetts 02111

Copyediting supervised by Barbara Sutton
Book production by Janet Z. Reynolds
Book design by Barbara Anderson

Typeset in 11 pt. Garamond
by Compset, Inc., Beverly, Massachusetts

Printed on permanent/durable acid-free paper
and bound in the United States of America

First published 1990.
10 9 8 7 6 5 4 3 2 1

Library of Congress Cataloging-in-Publication Data

McWilliams, Dean.
    John Gardner / by Dean McWilliams.
        p.   cm.—(Twayne's United States authors series ; TUSAS 561)
    Includes bibliographical references.
    ISBN 0-8057-7602-8 (alk. paper)
    1. Gardner, John, 1933–   —Criticism and interpretation.
    I. Title. II. Series.
    PS3557.A712Z77   1990
    813'.54—dc20   89-24648
                                                              CIP

For Alvi

Contents

About the Author
Preface
Acknowledgments
Chronology

Chapter One
Moral Fiction and Dialogical Form   1

Chapter Two
The Resurrection   10

Chapter Three
The Wreckage of Agathon   20

Chapter Four
Grendel   29

Chapter Five
The Sunlight Dialogues   42

Chapter Six
Jason and Medeia   53

Chapter Seven
Nickel Mountain   62

Chapter Eight
October Light   74

Chapter Nine
Freddy's Book   88

Chapter Ten
Mickelsson's Ghosts   101

Chapter Eleven
Stillness and Shadows   112

Notes and References   125
Selected Bibliography   128
Index   131

About the Author

Dean McWilliams studied at St. Mary's College of California, where he earned his B.A., at the Sorbonne, and at the University of Oregon, where he earned his Ph.D. in comparative literature. He is professor of English at Ohio University in Athens, where he has received several awards for outstanding undergraduate and graduate teaching. He has also taught at the Universidad Veracruzana in Jalapa, Mexico; at the Université de Toulouse–Le Mirail in France; and at De La Salle University in Manila, Philippines. He has lectured on American literature and film at universities in Canada, Great Britain, Austria, Romania, Kenya, Zambia, and Madagascar.

McWilliams is the author of *The Narratives of Michel Butor: The Writer as Janus* and the translator of Jean Weisgerber, *Faulkner and Dostoevsky: Influence and Confluence.* He has also published numerous articles on American and French literature and film.

Preface

John Gardner was one of the most remarkable individuals in recent American literary history. Remarkable, first of all, for his extraordinary energy. Throughout the seventies and into the early eighties Gardner presented us with at least one—and often three or four—volumes a year. When he died at the age of forty-nine in 1982, Gardner left behind a list of publications that included eight novels, two collections of short stories, an epic poem, a volume of lyric poetry, eight scholarly or critical books, five children's books, and five volumes of plays and opera libretti. In addition, his literary executors have recently brought into print two of the novels he left unfinished at his death. To all of this must be added Gardner's very active career as a university professor, literary performer, and peripatetic cultural gadfly.

Even more remarkable was the quality of the fiction. It is enormously enjoyable, full of memorable characters and lively incidents. Three of his novels were best-sellers, and all have found appreciative audiences. At the same time, this fiction revealed an impressive artistic sophistication, drawing on Gardner's seemingly encyclopedic knowledge of Western literature and on many of the literary innovations of the modernist masters. In 1976 Gardner won the National Book Critics Circle Award for Fiction, and all of his fiction has drawn the attention of literary scholars.

This remarkable young talent, able to reach a broad popular audience with a serious and technically innovative fiction, arrived on the American literary scene at a propitious moment. Many readers and teachers of American literature sensed something was not quite right with American fiction in the mid-1970s. Many of the major voices of the postwar period—Saul Bellow, Bernard Malamud, Norman Mailer, Ralph Ellison, Eudora Welty—were still with us, but some of these were silent or nearly so and others seemed not to be working at the level of their previous achievement. In addition to these artists, whom we might call the late modernists, there was a younger generation that had emerged in the sixties and early seventies. Critics had high hopes for one tendency among these writers, called postmodernism, practiced by John Barth, William Gass, Donald Barthelme, Robert Coover, Thomas Pynchon, Stanley Elkin, and others.

Postmodernism carried to its logical conclusion the effort, initiated by Flaubert and continued by modernists such as Proust, Mann, Joyce, and Faulkner, to transform the novel, a popular mass entertainment in its origins, to a high art object. Postmodernists de-emphasized the creation of realistic setting, believable characters, and an emotionally engaging story. They emphasized instead the artificiality and the artistry of their creations through self-reflexive commentary, wordplay, and elements that deliberately disrupted the mimetic illusion. Many of us initially welcomed this witty, playful, and inventive writing, which provided a salutary contrast to the ponderous sobriety of much realist and modernist writing. Despite our initial enthusiasm, some of us discovered that these fictions did not bring us back for second or third readings. These ingenious verbal puzzles, once solved, could be put away in a drawer and forgotten. The postmodernist performances seemed more like ice dancing—skilled, intricately planned athletic exercises—than like ballet, whose distinctive conjunction of movement, music, and narrative touches us at a deeper, more resonant level.

Gardner's novels—especially *Nickel Mountain, October Light,* and *Grendel*—arrived like a fresh country breeze into the airless academic cloisters of contemporary fiction. These fictions were inventive, funny, and fully aware of where modernism had led the novel, and yet they were full of memorable characters and events. Moreover, they addressed compelling human issues, such as freedom and responsibility. It seemed to many observers that Gardner might help lead serious fiction out of the academy and back to a broader audience. Thus when it was announced that Gardner was preparing a major book-length critical statement, many of us were hopeful. Unfortunately, those hopes were disappointed. That statement, *On Moral Fiction,* published in 1978, is seriously flawed. It is misguided in its basic assumptions, poorly reasoned in its argument, and mean-spirited in tone. In it Gardner calls for an art that will offer positive models for emulation and attacks all those whose art he believes does not meet this test. He angrily points his finger at virtually everyone of consequence in contemporary American fiction and, his ire still unspent, he swings away at contemporary critics, composers, and visual artists as well. Gardner repeated his charges on television, radio, and on the lecture circuit, and he met his friend William Gass, a leading postmodernist, in debate in this country and in Europe. Many popular and scholarly publications reviewed the book—often hostilely; writers were queried on their reactions; and *Fiction International* put out a special issue[1] with the book as its focus.

In the admittedly rarefied world of American letters, *On Moral Fiction* was a media event.

Sadly, the worst casualty of this whole controversy has been our understanding of John Gardner's achievement. Despite its many weaknesses, *On Moral Fiction* is quite possibly Gardner's best-known work. It is certainly the most commented upon. Robert Morace's bibliography of the criticism on Gardner lists more entries for this polemical volume that for any of his other works, even his best-selling novels. One realizes the book's full influence only when, in reading the criticism of Gardner's fiction, one discovers how often critics have tried to read the novels in terms of the "moral" theory. This is unfortunate. Gardner's fiction is too rich, complex, and ambivalent—in short, too good—to fit comfortably within the poorly conceived strictures developed in his critical book. It is not so much that the "moral fiction" readings of Gardner's novels are *wrong*—Gardner, in one of his numerous voices, really did want to write uplifting stories. It is just that they are *partial* and tend to muffle the many other voices—some of them doubting and even nihilistic—echoing in his fictional world.

My purpose in this study is to help us to hear these other voices and to confront the unresolved tensions among them. In so doing I make use of the ideas of the Soviet theoretician Mikhail M. Bakhtin. Bakhtin's theories of polyphony and dialogic form, which I discuss in chapter 1, offer, it seems to me, a more adequate framework for describing Gardner's complex vision than do the ideas presented in *On Moral Fiction*.

Dean McWilliams

Ohio University

Acknowledgments

I am grateful to Ohio University for a Faculty Fellowship that gave me a year's leave during which I prepared the final draft of my study and for a Research Committee grant that helped me to purchase some of the books required for my research. My thanks also to Nancy Crampton who supplied the handsome portrait of John Gardner displayed on the dust jacket and as the frontispiece. Finally, I with to thank Warren French, editor of this series, for his encouragement, friendship, and judicious editorial counsel.

Chronology

1933   John Champlin Gardner, Jr., born 21 July, in Batavia, New York, the eldest of four children to John Champlin, a dairy farmer and a lay preacher, and Priscilla (Jones) Gardner, an English teacher.

1945   Accidentally kills his brother Gilbert in a farm accident.

1951   Graduates from Batavia High School and enters DePauw University in Greencastle, Indiana.

1953   Marries Joan Louise Patterson, his second cousin, and transfers to Washington University in St. Louis, Missouri.

1955   Graduates, is elected to Phi Beta Kappa and awarded a Woodrow Wilson Fellowship.

1958   Awarded Ph.D. from the University of Iowa. His graduate program combines medieval studies and creative writing. His Ph.D. dissertation is a novel, "The Old Men."

1958–1959   Teaches at Oberlin College in Oberlin, Ohio.

1959–1962   Teaches at Chico State College in Chico, California. Among his students is the writer Raymond Carver.

1962–1965   Teaches at San Francisco State College.

1965   Publishes *The Complete Works of the Gawain Poet*. Begins teaching at Southern Illinois University in Carbondale, Illinois.

1966   *The Resurrection*.

1970   *The Wreckage of Agathon*.

1971   *Grendel*.

1972   *The Sunlight Dialogues*.

1973   *Jason and Medeia* and *Nickel Mountain*.

1974   *The King's Indian Stories and Tales*. Teaches summer course at the Bread Loaf Writer's Conference in Middlebury, Vermont. Begins teaching at Bennington College, in Bennington, Vermont.

1976   *October Light.*

1977   Wins National Book Critics Circle Award for Fiction for *October Light.* Publishes *The Poetry of Chaucer* and *The Life and Times of Chaucer.* Separates from his wife. Enters hospital for cancer surgery.

1978   *On Moral Fiction.* Extensive lecturing, debates, and interviews to explain and defend the ideas in this book. Minor controversy results when reviewers criticize use of other scholars without appropriate acknowledgment in his Chaucer biography. Accepts teaching position with the State University of New York at Binghamton. Marries Liz Rosenberg.

1980   *Freddy's Book.*

1981   *The Art of Living and Other Stories.*

1982   *Mickelsson's Ghosts.* Divorces Liz Rosenberg. Dies in motorcycle accident 14 September, less than a week prior to his planned marriage to Susan Thornton.

1986   Publication of *"Stillness" and "Shadows",* two manuscripts left uncompleted at Gardner's death.

Chapter One
Moral Fiction and Dialogical Form

Gardner intended *On Moral Fiction* to be a call for "moral art," that is, art that "has a clear positive moral effect, presenting valid models for imitation, eternal verities worth keeping in mind, and a benevolent vision of the possible which can inspire and incite human beings toward virtue, toward life affirmation as opposed to destruction or indifference."[1] These are laudable goals, and Gardner offers worthwhile comments, but these are obscured by mistakes in argument and tone that are evident already in the first paragraph. That paragraph introduces Gardner's controlling metaphor—the hammer of Thor, the Norse god of thunder. The symbol was dear to Gardner, a medievalist by training, who considered using it as the title for his book and who returned to it frequently in his critical writing and interviews. Gardner explains that in the old days Thor drew a circle around Middle Earth, marking the territory that he would defend and beating back the enemies of order with his hammer. Gradually, however, Thor grew older and weaker, and the circle grew smaller until finally Thor disappeared:

All we have left is Thor's hammer, which represents not brute force but art, or, counting both hammerheads, art and criticism. Thor is no help. Like other gods, he has withdrawn from our immediate view. We have only his weapon, abandoned beside a fencepost in high weeds, if we can figure out how to use it. This book is an attempt to develop a set of instructions, an analysis of what has gone wrong in recent years with the various arts—especially fiction, since that is the art on which I'm best informed—and what has gone wrong with criticism. (3–4)

The Failure of *On Moral Fiction*

Gardner's instruction book fails because he ignores fundamental contradictions in his controlling metaphor and in his own approach.

The difficulty is not so much knowing *how to defend* as it is knowing *what to defend*. We do not need instructions in how to swing the moral hammer—Americans are world champions in *that* event—but we are deeply confused and divided about where to stand when we do so. For Thor the problem of where to place one's feet was much less problematic; he had divine wisdom, and, moreover, the place where the god stood was, by definition, holy. But, as Gardner freely admits, the twilight came, Thor disappeared, and the sun set on the theocentric worldview that made such combative moral confidence possible. We now find ourselves alone in the dark with no sure moral footing.

Gardner's problem in this manifesto is that he wants to create and criticize art according to the universally applicable moral principles that were possible when we enjoyed a consensus on these issues. But, as Gardner's fiction shows us, the religious and philosophical underpinnings of such a consensus crumbled long ago. How, in our modern metaphysical darkness, can an artist discover and argue definitions of "moral," "good," and "life-affirming" that represent more than his or her subjective predilections?

Gardner struggles with this problem in the second chapter of his book. His heroes—Homer, Dante, Chaucer, and Tolstoy—stand on the other side of the historical division between faith and unbelief. Gardner discusses the romantic artists who took us across this divide. These artists knew, in the wake of the Enlightenment, revolution, and industrial dislocation, that the world had changed. They sought simultaneously to become the gods who legislate models of behavior, the heroes who embody these models, and the singers who memorialize them. They did so in the belief that they were not acting exclusively on private impulse but that they were in contact with the divine—now understood variously as nature or human love. But most modern writers cannot accept even this attenuated form of religious faith, and Gardner does not say that they are wrong. What Gardner does say is that, despite much cynicism, "the moral position is still popular with writers, however loudly they may claim it's not so: art instructs" (39). What Gardner does not prove—granting for a moment his judgment on his colleagues' bad faith—is that such a moral position is justified. How, again, does an artist living in a relativistic world discover and defend a universally applicable moral position?

Gardner's nostalgia for the romantic artist is both ironic and perfectly understandable because, as Gerald Graff as shown,[2] this artist is the ultimate source for the problems carried to their logical conclusion in postmodernism. The romantic poet—"mighty prophet, seerblest"—sought to step in and create a vision that would replace the decaying religious and political foundations of authority. Unfortunately, this gesture carried within it the seeds of its own destruction, for the romantic notion of an autonomous creative imagination, in effect, conceded that its creation must necessarily be the arbitrary, subjective product of a single consciousness. As long as some gossamer remnants of the old worldview survived, artists could hope that their personal insights were somehow linked to a deeper divine principle. But once these final veils blew away late in the nineteenth century, the artist was naked. Postmodernists like John Barth and William Gass have been rigorously consistent, acknowledging and even flaunting their nudity. They argue that the artist's only intellectually honest position is to admit that he or she can offer nothing more than a private opinion, words on a page, not eternal truths.

Gardner, for his part, will not give over easily to this position and tries to rescue the romantic posture. In chapter 3 he takes up the romantic notion of the poet-priest. He explains that although art and religion were once joined in our culture, they are now very separate things. Nonetheless, Gardner wants to keep an analogy between the two. Here is an example of his confusion on this point: "The articulation which satisfies an artist is directly analogous to that which satisfies a preacher: an interpretation of the experience of his own time and place, summed up in the person of the artist or preacher, developed through the medium of the whole tradition, of, in one case, art, and in the other case, doctrine" (166–67). The comparison ignores the very different resources available to the artist and to the preacher. Both, it is true, draw on tradition, and perhaps Gardner means to suggest that these traditions can, in art as in religion, provide a sure guide to what is moral and immoral. But this overlooks the important differences between the two contrasting forms of tradition. Religious tradition, for believers within a given confession, is essentially ahistorical and homogeneous: although there may be differences of emphasis between different periods and different individuals, the central tenets are divinely revealed, eternal truths accepted by all members of the confession. Literary tradition, on the other hand, is historical and heterogeneous: it is constantly evolving, often in dramatic reversals, and it consists, at any given moment, of many loudly contending schools. Thus, while a theologian can decide fairly easily whether a teaching is immoral within a given confession, about all a literary historian can tell us is whether a work conforms to the norms of a given period, genre, or movement.

The question of tradition raises the issue of the temporal status of art's moral truths. Sometimes Gardner argues that they are "eternal verities" (18, 82), and that the artist cannot pander to his time (169). But he concedes elsewhere that "Truth is relative in the same manner as is Goodness" (140). Trying to square the circle, he decides that these truths are "approximately absolute at any given point in time but relative with respect to the total history of mankind" (134). How does one discover "the approximate absolute" of one's time? Are there objective proofs, or are there only subjective preferences? We are told that "true art treats ideals, affirming and clarifying the Good, the True and the Beautiful" (133). But if we think that these capitalized concepts, marching bravely across the page, will lead us to objective standards, we are mistaken. The final test is subjective: if the reader "finds the so-called art 'creepy'—then the artist's creative energy is misspent" (180). Most artists and critics will find this "creepiness test" singularly inadequate for making broad discriminations between moral and immoral art.

Unfortunately, Gardner does not allow the fact that he is up to his ankles in philosophical quicksand to prevent him from swinging his hammer. For the moralizing Gardner surveying all the contemporary arts, virtually everything is "tinny and commercial and often, in addition, hollow and academic" (5). John Updike, John Barth, and Thomas Pynchon, he declares, "will die of intellectual blight, academic narrowness, or fakery" (94). Gardner goes on to detail the sins of Saul Bellow, Bernard Malamud, Norman Mailer, John Cheever, Katherine Anne Porter, Walker Percy, Joseph Heller, Harry Crews, Anne Tyler, E. L. Doctorow, Stanley Elkin, William Gass, Frederick Buechner, Robert Coover, and Donald Barthelme. It is true that Gardner makes concessions to some of these writers and praises others, although those he praises are fewer and generally less known than those he censures. Adding to all of this, of course, was the implication, carried in the book's title and central argument, that these criticisms were ethical as well artistic. John Barth summarized the impression many carried from their reading of *On Moral Fiction* when he described the book as "an exercise in literary kneecapping."[3]

Gardner's Other Voices

Much more consequential than the bruised feelings of his colleagues was the blow Gardner's book dealt to the understanding of his own work, for *On Moral Fiction* provides a singularly limited and unreliable description of the purposes and practices embodied in Gardner's novels. Gardner, in fact, describes those purposes elsewhere in terms that directly contradict the terms espoused in his manifesto. In his critical book he attacked the postmodernists for turning their back on the real world and caring only for literary form, but, in earlier interviews he characterized his own fiction as pure style, with nothing to say, aligning himself solidly with the postmodernists he was later to attack. In 1971 he told Digby Diehl: "I have nothing to say, except that I think words are beautiful. I'm a stylist; for me, everything is rhythm and rhyme. There are a handful of other stylists like Gass, Elkin, Barthelme, Barth and Ralph Ellison who have nothing to say either. We just write."[4] In 1974 he made a similar statement to Joe David Bellamy and again identified himself with the postmodernists: "That's what I think fiction now is about. It's about creating circus sideshows. I *don't* think they're trivial. I think anybody who writes the way us guys write is going to be at the mercy of the critics. . . . I mean Stanley Elkin, Bill Gass, Donald Barthelme. . . . I don't know if they would be happy to be linked with me; so, you know, all apologies to them for my putting myself in their company. But I think they are fundamentally people making sideshows—but good, serious sideshows, because they raise you to your best, *not* philosophically, *not* morally."[5]

One might argue that the differences between the earlier statements and the 1978 critical book result from a development in Gardner's thinking: Gardner, according to this explanation, began as a postmodernist, remained one through the mid-1970s, and converted to moralism in the late seventies. But Gardner has insisted that *On Moral Fiction* represents long-held artistic beliefs. He began it in 1964, well before his first novel was published, and his early drafts were even angrier than the version that he toned down for the 1978 publication.[6] Gardner did not lie in any of these statements, and he did not go through any radical conversion experience. These differing statements bring us to something that is absolutely crucial for understanding Gardner's personal psychology and his fictional practice. John Gardner was capable of holding and operating on different, even contradictory, intellectual propositions at the same time and in the same work. Rather than confusion, this intellectual elasticity and tolerance produced the marvelous richness and complexity that distinguishes his best fiction.

We get a sense of this elasticity in *On Moral Fiction* where we can hear, if we listen closely, another Gardner, only partially obscured by the table-pounding moralizer. This Gardner, enormously sensitive to life's complexity and ambiguities, eschews didacticism. He insists that an artist cannot start out with an unalterable conception of the meaning that his fiction will eventually yield. The artist discovers that meaning by placing ideas and values in a dramatic context, setting them against other ideas and values, and testing them all in action. The commitment to honest, fair-minded exploration of these materials "forces the writer to intense yet dispassionate and unprejudiced watchfulness, drives him—in ways abstract logic cannot match—to unexpected discoveries and, frequently, a change of mind" (108).

Gardner goes on to state that he began *October Light* as a celebration of the traditional values embodied by James Page, a son of Thor who wields a shotgun instead of a hammer. The actual writing of the novel, however, committed Gardner to testing those values by placing them in action and in conflict with other values; this testing led to a resolution significantly different from the one Gardner had anticipated. The novel's richness results from the fact that we hear James's voice in concert with at least a half dozen other voices that challenge, modify, and amplify the issues in a complex dialogue.

The process that Gardner describes in his creation of *October Light* resembles the process of moral evaluation of literature that Wayne Booth describes in *The Company We Keep: An Ethics of Fiction*. Booth's central comparison—present in his book's title—is between choosing our human and our literary friends; he suggests that "we arrive at our sense of value in narratives in precisely the way we arrive at our sense of value in persons: by *experiencing* them in an immeasurably rich context of others that are both like and unlike them."[7] The process in both instances is gradual and comparative, requiring us to place our new human or literary acquaintance against other such acquaintances. It is also, in a sense, "experimental," in that it requires us to observe the consequences of this company-keeping on our own sensibilities, and it is social, since we often share our impression of these encounters with others and learn from this exchange. Finally, the principles from which we work are constantly evolving, for each new acquaintance and judgment can alter or modify previous judgments.

This process is difficult, but it is all the more valuable for that. It is precisely because we do not possess a set of certain, a priori ethical postulates that we must acquaint ourselves with the moral universe in this gradual, experimental fashion. It also explains what, for Booth, is "the unique value of fiction: its relative cost-free offer of trial runs. If you try out a given mode of life in itself, you may, like Eve in the garden, discover too late that the one who offered it to you was Old Nick himself. Though tryings-out in narrative present all the dangers we have stressed throughout, they offer both a relative freedom from consequence, and in their sheer multiplicity, a rich supply of antidotes.[8] I am grateful for Booth's discussion, for it takes seriously the ethical implications of our reading, without calling for a flat-footed defense of traditional moral turf. On the contrary, it values an adventurous spirit that explores and tries out different approaches.

Gardner and Bakhtin's Dialogical Form

In describing the way in which Gardner's *October Light* tests various moral positions I spoke of the dialogue that it creates among them. The term *dialogue* has been given new emphasis and meaning by the critical writings of the Soviet theorist Mikhail M. Bakhtin, and I believe Bakhtin's ideas help us to understand the structure and function of Gardner's fiction. For Bakhtin the history of literary narrative reveals two contrasting tendencies, which are found in all periods but which tend to dominate in one period or another. The first of these is centripetal and monological: all meaning is absorbed into and controlled by a single, all-encompassing value system. The other is centrifugal and dialogical: meaning explodes outward into a multiplicity of contending worldviews, all of which are given a fair hearing. The first tendency is seen most clearly in the epic, a narrative set in a world qualitatively different and temporally remote from our own. The heroes of this world are animated by the universally acknowledged values of the culture, which the epic celebrates. The hero has only to follow his code: the answers are ready, latent in the norms of the culture, before the questions are posed. The epic narrator is there, above the action, commenting and directing, to make certain that these norms are understood and embraced by the epic audience.

The second tendency—seen in the novel and preeminently in the greatest novels—emerges in the late Renaissance as the religious and philosophical consensus enjoyed by the classic and Christian epic disintegrates. The time is the present in all its immediacy, confusion, and open-endedness. The inhabitants of this world are driven by private motives and animated by contrasting and competing worldviews. The novel form allows them free rein to develop their views and to act on them. It does not constrain them to embrace the values of the narrator, who may, in fact, simply be another one of the characters. At its best the novel can be a true dialogue: "a plurality of independent and unmerged voices and consciousnesses, a genuine polyphony of fully valid voices."[9]

Gardner's narratives, I believe, offer such a polyphony. One bears *dialogue* in its title, and all are dialogical in the sense we have defined above. Each of these narratives presents a range of characters animated by contrasting sets of values. Some of these characters are torn by conflicting ideologies and are thus the scene of wrenching internal dialogues. Each of the characters is allowed to expatiate, sometimes noisily, his or her point of view and forced to consider the ideas of others. All of these values are tested in the working out of the novel's plot. No clear "winners" emerge from these dialogues, nor should an uncritical reading of *On Moral Fiction* force us into crowning one. Certain values, it is true, will prove, in the course of the developing conflict, to be better adapted to certain situations. But Gardner's resolutions, particularly the endings of his narratives, are notoriously ambiguous and open ended. Thus we must continue to listen to the dialogue, to hear how contrasting voices and reverberations from the dramatic context challenge, qualify, and modify even those voices with which we most identify.

Meaning in Gardner's novels, as in the greatest fiction, does not emerge from a single voice but from a dialogue between voices. The meaning is that dialogue—not the victory of one voice over another, but the tension between them, the texture of a world where competing visions of the world must coexist: Ivan and Alyosha and Dmitri; Stephen and Bloom and Molly; Quentin and Jason and Dilsey. This is not, however, mere relativism. As the voices are developed and tested in the narrative, rough hierarchies will emerge: Alyosha will seem, to many readers, preferable to Ivan, Bloom to Stephen, and Dilsey to Jason. And yet none of these represents a final answer; none is allowed, in our world, to stand alone. They must always be complemented, challenged, and corrected by competing views. Criticism diminishes the richness of these fictions when it imposes a monological reading, and it also negates one of the novel's great values for us. It is precisely because we do not inhabit Thor's world and, thus, do not have a single notion of the moral that we need great novels. Our individual perspectives are always limited, distorted by the arbitrary, fragmentary nature of language itself. The novel developed, Bakhtin explains, to accommodate our evolving, ideologically heterogeneous condition. It permits several perspectives, enables us to see from different angles, and provides a model for a dialogical consciousness that is alive to life's ambiguity without lapsing into despairing relativism.

Gardner's criticism, like his fiction, is inhabited by numerous voices. I have already mentioned another voice, more reasonable than the irascible troll policeman, who can be heard in *On Moral Fiction*. This voice becomes more audible in Gardner's last critical writings. I would like to conclude this introduction with the definition of the literary artist that he offered in his posthumous advice to young writers. It suggests, I believe, the sensitive, tolerant, and generous spirit that we find in his fiction:

The writer must be not only capable of understanding people different from himself but fascinated by such people. He must have sufficient self-esteem that he is not threatened by difference, and sufficient warmth and sympathy, and a sufficient concern with fairness, that he wants to value people different from himself, and finally he must have, I think, sufficient faith in the goodness of life that he can not only tolerate but celebrate a world of differences, conflicts, oppositions. [10]

Chapter Two
The Resurrection

The title of Gardner's first published novel (1966)—the first words we encounter when we enter his novelistic universe chronologically—contains one of the most suggestive and significant words in his canon. *Resurrection*: the noun, in our Christian culture, inevitably evokes Jesus' triumphant stepping forth from the grave and his promise that his believers might know the same experience. Thus its first connotation is religious, a rebirth into a new spiritual existence after death. Closely related to this is a second, moral connotation, the possibility of rebirth in this world, a sloughing off of an inauthentic mode of existence for one more profound and more fulfilling. Gardner returns continually in his fiction to variations of this second connotation, for it embodies a crucial moral question: can humans actually control their behavior, can they change and be morally reborn. Although Gardner places primary emphasis on this secular meaning, the religious meaning is never completely forgotten. Gardner's characters constantly wonder about and hunger for a spiritual dimension that would provide the energy for moral reform.

In this novel death provides the immediate context and gives particular urgency to the issues raised by its title. James Chandler, a middle-aged philosophy professor, discovers that he has incurable leukemia and that he has only a few weeks to live. The novel is the story of those final weeks in the lives of Chandler, his family, and his acquaintances. Their thoughts and actions provide a rich dialogue on the problems of moral resurrection.

The Question of Rebirth

The question of rebirth is articulated explicitly by John Horne, Chandler's fellow patient in a Batavia, New York, hospital. Horne, a legal clerk and an amateur philosopher, traps Chandler's wife in a fevered philosophical monologue, during the course of which he asks, "Is it possible for a man to be reborn?"[1] Horne's concern is not physical death—his illness is minor—rather he wishes to escape the moral death he feels that he is living. Horne has surveyed the motives for his own behavior and that of others he has known, and he finds only self-love. He would like to escape this egoism and change his life, but he denies that he, or any other human, has the power to do so. For Horne, such dramatic change comes not from personal choice but from powerful forces outside the individual; individual humans do not control their moral destinies.

Horne knows Chandler's philosophical work and eagerly pursues him with the same questions he posed to Chandler's wife. Horne gets no answer, and he does not manage to change his life. His self-absorption is too complete, and his questioning too obsessive for him ever to change his behavior and authentically reach out to another. He, in fact, never manages a true dialogue with either of the Chandlers; he simply treats them as sounding boards for his harangues, and, not surprisingly, they become bored and avoid him. We last see Horne in the novel's penultimate chapter, lecturing a blind old woman in a hospital hallway. The more he talks—mentioning Saint Francis, Hitler, Epictetus, and Marx along the way—the more confused he becomes. He eventually comes, in this monologue, to doubt consciousness itself. Horne's indefatigable questioning erodes each of the theories he throws up, trapping him in an endless monologue that drives away the very humans—James Chandler in particular—with whom he most wishes to make contact. Thus we discover in Horne the conflicting pressures—moral stasis versus moral rebirth, intellectual analysis versus direct emotional involvement—that rend many of the novel's characters.

James Chandler also struggles with these issues. He has spent his adult life as a professional philosopher, but he discovers that his imminent death casts an ironic light over this work. His epistemological monograph "Am I Dreaming?" was a rather whimsical intellectual joke, but in his final weeks he will become increasingly troubled by the nightmares that disturb his sleep. Do these dreams, he wonders, presage a spiritual realm beyond the material one? Similarly, he has been planning a major metaphysical statement that assumes that the large questions this discipline traditionally addressed no longer trouble modern man, but he now finds that these issues are urgently relevant to his personal condition. Chandler the professional philosopher had fled "into the comforting arms of pedantic abstraction" (13), but his death sentence breaks this comfortable complacency and forces him to decide how he will live his final days. He will be torn in these hours between a desire to continue his intellectual work and a wish to restore emotional contact with his family.

Chandler's first impulse is to abandon philosophy, which he now sees as meaningless, and to try to live as intensely as possible. He will "seize existence by the scrotum" and return to the existentialism of his youth: "For if Heidegger refused to ask ultimate questions, refused to acknowledge that the answers to one's immediate questions might well be involved with larger answers, at least such a man could say, like Gide's Thésée, *J'ai vécu!*" (43). Chandler is undoubtedly sincere, but we should note that, even in this philosophical leavetaking, he has to refer to Heidegger and to quote Gide in French. We might suspect that the issue is far from resolved, and subsequent events will justify this suspicion.

Chandler attempts to carry out his new resolve by returning with his family to his hometown and to his mother with whom he has had little contact during his years as a professional philosopher. He tries to communicate with his wife and three daughters, but his efforts are clumsy and end in frustration. Chandler's illness worsens, and he ends up in a hospital, where, to his relief, he can return to his philosophical speculations. One line of these speculations is initiated by the continual appearance in his dreams of a mysterious old woman, who seems to be a messenger from the world of spirit. Chandler becomes obsessed by this woman, particularly after he believes that he glimpses her when he is awake: if she actually exists this would, for Chandler, imply a world beyond the one we know with our senses. He sets about to explore the question in a systematic, philosophical fashion and tortures the problem for many hours. He finally realizes, however, that such analysis is futile and surrenders to his experience, accepting the woman "in courtesy and peace" (166).

Making Life Art

Chandler's acceptance of his spiritual encounter frees his mind for another problem, which enters almost immediately upon the previous one. Chandler has experienced a strange emotion in the presence of a painting by Aunt Emma Staley, who may be the old lady of his dreams. While contemplating this scrupulously detailed rendering of an old mill, Chandler feels stirred by a strange exhilaration mixed with a profound dissatisfaction with his life. Later he realizes that painting represents for him "the soul's sublime acceptance of lawless, proliferating substance" (166–167). Stimulated by these reflections, Chandler uses a good portion of his remaining strength to sketch out what he believes will be a major breakthrough in aesthetics. These reflections are interrupted as they are nearing completion by a surprising declaration: Viola Staley, teenage companion to the elderly Staley sisters, suddenly professes her love to Chandler. Chandler responds awkwardly to the young woman, who flees in embarrassment, but he has been deeply shaken. This unexpected confrontation with strong feeling awakens him once again to the fact that his aesthetic speculations have cut him off from the real world: "it was not the beauty of the world one must affirm but *the world,* the buzzing blooming confusion itself. He had slipped from celebrating what was to the celebration of empty celebration. . . . *One must make life art*" (229). Thus, both lines of Chandler's philosophical enquiry—the reality of the mysterious woman and the meaning of art—lead him away from abstract thought and back to the immediate life of the senses and feeling.

To crown this recognition, Chandler uses what are probably the final moments of his life to pursue Viola and to try to speak to her. Chandler manages, it seems, to do what Horne could not do, that is, to change his life and be reborn in love. The dramatic context of Chandler's final gesture, however, prevents us from giving it an easy, romantic reading. Chandler crawls across a urine-stained carpet, blood flowing from his nose, and clutches at Viola's bare foot. Viola gives no sign of recognition. This strange scene seems to leave open as many questions as it answers. Chandler does feel a powerful emotion—probably love—but would it endure if he were allowed to live? Would he be able to live out his new commitment to others, or would he lapse back, as he did earlier, to his old habits? These are some of the issues that remain unresolved in James Chandler's resurrection.

Rebirth in Other Characters

The novel's title also refers to the dramatic change in Viola Staley's life. At the novel's outset, she is living a spiritual death much deeper than James Chandler's and, in fact, even yearns for physical death. Orphaned and raised by three eccentric maiden aunts, Viola has never had a real family nor a real childhood. The Chandlers, whom she meets when James visits the Staleys, seem to represent all that she has missed. She plunges into the life of this family, caring for the three daughters as Marie Chandler attends to her husband at the hospital. And yet there is something disturbing about Viola's devotion. She dissembles to ingratiate herself with the Chandlers, and she creates a romantic image of James that has little to do with the real man. She does manage, it is true, to declare her love and to help James break out of his self-absorption. We must note, however, that to do so she abandons her aunt who, in Viola's absence, wanders off, perhaps to her death. Viola most certainly does change her life, but the meaning of that change, as with James, is far from clear.

James Chandler's drama effects changes in other members of his family, including his mother. Rose Chandler is, in many ways, the opposite of her son, for she has always lived in the moment, "drinking deep of the present, not tasting and hurrying on" (188). The imminent death of one she loves, however, prods her to consider larger speculative questions and to envy the philosopher's perspective. She falls into a discussion of these questions with an old farmer, who offers what he has learned in more than a half century's reflections: "Everything in this world was made to go to waste, ma'am. . . . Only real difference between people and trees is trees don't fret about it. People ought to be more like trees, Mrs. Chandler. That's my philosophy" (197–98). Rose Chandler regards her interlocutor critically and rejects his homely, naturalistic wisdom: "People aren't supposed to be trees, Mr. Plumber" (198). If we are tempted to exaggerate the moral implicit in James Chandler's turn from philosophy, we must deal with the counterexample of his mother, who is moving in the other direction. Rose Chandler's voice in this dialogue reminds us that it is basic to our identity as humans to "fret" about life's meaning.

James's eldest daughter, Karen, although only eight years old, feels the need her grandmother has defended. During her father's illness, she drags a heavy tome—Immanuel Kant's *Critique of Pure Reason*—from beneath her bedcovers and asks Viola's help in reading it. Later, after hearing a romantic but improbable story of an Indian couple's tragic love, she asks, "There *is* no God, is there, Viola?" Viola can only respond, *"Nobody knows"* (218).

Karen has been changed by her father's illness and death and will bear the effects of this change the rest of her life. The one member of the family who manages to pass through this ordeal relatively unchanged is Marie, James's wife. Marie has little interest in the speculative questions that absorb her husband, his colleagues, and his students. James tends to patronize her, but he recognizes that her view of the world—intuitive and unsystematic though it may be—is profound. James recalls a moment earlier in their marriage when, after visiting a sculpture exhibition, they sat with two friends on a cliff overlooking the Pacific. The others energetically dispute the significance of the art they have seen until Marie interrupts them, gesturing and speaking with conviction:

"This is much truer—whatever that may mean." All three of them looked at the same time, as if perfectly understanding her, at the miles of gray-green, dwarfish trees, the cliffs to the right, the ocean falling away to Japan, the wide storm of birds. What Chandler, at least, had seen that instant was Death, wheeling and howling, and two little girls in red coats running down the path toward them, laughing. Marie sat like the Buddha, her legs out like sticks, her red hands resting tranquilly on her enormous belly. Her face was full of light. (155)

Marie, as we see her here, offers, fleetingly, the closest thing we get to a moral center in the novel. Looking out at sea, addressing her friends, she embraces the moment, with a full understanding of its inevitable passing. Less speculative than James, more profound than Rose, she manages, for an instant at least, the conflicting forces struggling within these other characters.

Opaque Epiphanies

James and the reader experience an authentic epiphany in this instant: we assist at a moment when an important truth is revealed in a striking, emblematic scene. James and the reader discover the beauty and profundity of Marie's acceptance of the world. Moments such as these occur in Gardner's fiction, but they are rare. Much more typical are moments that might be described as opaque epiphanies. The latter instances resemble the scene on the cliff in that they are visually striking, emotionally moving experiences that seem to promise some deep insight. These opaque epiphanies differ from the moment on the cliff, however, in that they remain hauntingly mysterious, troubling the thoughts of the characters and of the reader, without ever allowing themselves to be reduced to a clear insight of the type James articulates about Marie. Such frustrated epiphanies are characteristic of Gardner's complex moral vision, and they are crucial to his dialogical form. These scenes punctuate the quests undertaken by Gardner's protagonists, sometimes forming minor climaxes in the narratives and frequently providing the final scene. They suggest a number of possible meanings, but it is rare that they can be subsumed by any single meaning. Thus, rather than ending the search, they keep it open, forcing us to attend to a range of possible meanings.

There are a number of such scenes in *The Resurrection*. One occurs early on when James's daughters drag him away from his books to witness a baseball game played by blind students. The Chandlers stand transfixed, watching with fear and fascination, as the sightless children grope through the grass on their hands and knees, hunting their ball whose identifying bell has gone silent. The instant seems pregnant with significance—is it an emblem of the Chandlers' blind search for love and meaning? We are never told, and the mysterious scene will echo in our minds, unresolved, as we continue the narrative.

Another such moment will end the novel. Three events occur almost simultaneously and are narrated in the last three chapters. At the hospital John Horne continues a progressively less coherent philosophical meditation for his elderly interlocutor. At the Staley home, in Aunt Emma's bedroom, James Chandler reaches out to Viola Staley. Elsewhere in the same house, perhaps at the same moment, Aunt Betsy Staley prepares to play for the guests invited for her annual recital:

Aunt Betsy smiled and seated herself at the farther piano. Absolute silence. The silence lasted for nearly a minute, and then, with unbelievable power, there came four notes, a long pause, four more. Then there exploded a terrible holocaust of chords and runs, each note precise, overpowering, irremissible— not music but a monstrous retribution of sound, the mindless roar of things in motion, on the meddlesome mind of man. Karen said, "Mother, Miss Staley's *deaf*!" "Be still," she said. The people sat listening, perfectly silent, as if deeply impressed, staring at their knees. And whether or not they knew what was it was they were witnessing, no stranger could have said. (243–44)

Thus ends the novel. An appropriate ending for a novel whose key scenes, like James's haunting dreams, seem luminous with portentous meaning but deliberately leave us just this side of an articulation of that meaning.

Gardner Answers Tolstoy

James Chandler, as we have said, uses some of his final hours to develop a theory of art. It will be helpful for understanding the function and structure of Gardner's novels to consider this theory. Chandler objects to Kant's separation of the aesthetic from the ethical. For Chandler, the artistic experience does not exclude the moral experience but rather includes it and transcends it. The goal of art, he argues, is "aesthetic wholeness" (202), a state of consciousness that embraces all of our experience, including the moral, but that does so selflessly. In developing his theory, Chandler indicates how art has a practical effect in our moral growth. In our ethical lives we are constantly learning to categorize and choose between conflicting alternatives; our aesthetic encounters aid us in this, for "in Art a gifted consciousness simplifies, extends, or reorders categorization and choice for the rest of us, speeding up the painfully slow process of evolution toward what, hopefully, we *are*" (202). This formulation, I believe, provides a fair description of what takes place in this novel and in all of Gardner's dialogical fiction. The novel organizes a range of responses to pressing moral issues and allows us to follow the consequences of these responses; in so doing it assists us in developing an ethical perspective that is more comprehensive, sensitive, and tolerant.

Gardner's fiction is moral in this broader sense, but it is not didactic. Gardner was quite clear about this distinction and, in fact, planned this work as a response to *Resurrection,* Tolstoy's most didactic novel. Gardner regarded this work as "an awful, awful, just wicked book,"[2] and he echoes its title in his own title, not to pay homage to it, but to call attention to the very different approach his own novel takes. A contrast of these two books will help us to see more clearly the thematic and structural implications of this approach for Gardner's own fiction. The comparison will be all the more useful in that Bakhtin frequently uses Tolstoy's fiction as an example of monological form, which he contrasts with the more authentically dialogical fiction of Dostoyevski.

Tolstoy begins his novel, after offering four quotes from the New Testament, by describing a spring morning. He shows us the sun warming the earth, the trees pushing forth their leaves, and the birds building their nests: "All were happy—plants, birds, insects and children. But grown-up people—adult men and women—never left off cheating and tormenting themselves and one another. It was not this spring morning which they considered sacred and important, not the beauty of God's world, given to all creatures to enjoy—a beauty which inclines the heart to peace, to harmony and to love. No, what they considered sacred and important were their own devices for wielding power over each other."[3] In his first paragraph Tolstoy introduces the point of view from which he will narrate his novel. The omniscient narrator describing and commenting on this landscape will be our constant companion and guide, describing the characters, summarizing their histories, and revealing their innermost thoughts. He knows more than any of the characters, knows their destinies and relates and filters everything according to the central drama, the moral regeneration of a young Russian nobleman. But he does more: he introduces the moral perspective—respect for the sacred forces in nature, the foundation of Tolstoy's Christian primitivism—by which the narrator will judge all the characters and institutions presented in the novel. Thus one voice, the narrator's, enjoys a privileged status, both intellectually and morally, and dominates all others in the novel's chorus. Because of the dominance of this single, authorial voice, Bakhtin describes Tolstoy's world as "monolithically monologic."[4]

Gardner, perhaps deliberately echoing Tolstoy, also begins the prologue of his novel with an omniscient narrator describing nature in spring. The setting is the graveyard in which James Chandler lies, and the meanings it suggests are mixed. The pastures surrounding the cemetery are smooth and parklike, but the creek that flows through them is like "yellow mercury" (1). The narrator calls our attention to two unchanging patterns: the first is the natural rebirth so evident in the spring; the second is decay—despite the seasonal renewal, the tombstones crumble and species disappear. But these rhythms seem remote from humankind. It is not merely that humans are indifferent, as they were for Tolstoy, but that these natural forces seem to occur on an entirely different level, "like sound waves on an empty planet" (1).

It is now at least ten years since James's death, and we see his grave and watch a succession of visitors to it over the years: Rose, Marie, Karen, and Viola. Karen recognizes and greets Viola, but she gets no response. The prologue concludes with this paragraph:

A tiresome business, from the point of view of the dead. Say it were not what we know it is, some trifling domestic tragedy, but something more grand— the fall of civilization, the end of the world, the death of all consciousness, or, to speak recklessly, the Second Coming! Not a dead eyebrow would rise. The dead might, perhaps, rise; but they would not be impressed. Burdocks have grown up along the fence, hiding in their musty darkness the neatly lettered but no longer legible sign, *Perpetual Care*. (3)

The novel's title, *The Resurrection*, echoes with conflicting connotations when read against this prologue. There is natural rebirth—the trees leafing out alongside the Tonawanda Creek prove it—and the dead are reborn in the memory of those they loved. And yet these momentary resurrections seem trivial balanced against the ultimate and total victory of death, decay, and entropy. In this latter context the novel's title and the prologue's final words—*Perpetual Care*—ring ironically. Gardner's prologue, in contrast to Tolstoy's morally unambiguous introduction, asserts a tension of conflicting meanings and possibilities within which the novel's characters will work out their destinies.

Gardner's narrator stands even further above the characters than does Tolstoy's: he sees the past as well as the future, but withdraws and does not deign to enter the minds of the characters. He does, it is true, embody a distinct moral attitude—a world-weary indifference. But, after the prologue, this voice withdraws, and the novel's focus changes. The body of the novel consists of three parts, each of which contains twelve chapters. With only minor exceptions, each chapter will be focused through a single character's consciousness. All of part 1 is focused through James Chandler; in the first chapter the narrator retains a certain distance, but in subsequent chapters he will submerge himself almost entirely in James's point of view. The chapters of part 2 offer the perspectives of three characters: James, Marie, and Viola. Part 3 expands to six perspectives: the three mentioned above plus Horne, Rose, and a neutral perspective that sees several characters from outside. Thus the focus gradually moves away from the protagonist, exploring other characters and other consciousnesses, as it works changes and variations on the themes the protagonist's story has introduced. Each of these characters is permitted to develop and live out his or her values in relative autonomy and without intrusion or comment by a censorious narrator.

Bakhtin's description of the dialogical author, written to describe Dostoyevski and to contrast him with Tolstoy, can be applied here:

The author's consciousness does not transform others' consciousnesses (that is, the consciousnesses of the characters) into objects, and does not give them secondhand and finalizing definitions. Alongside and in front of itself it senses others' equally valid consciousnesses, just as infinite and open-ended as itself. It reflects and re-creates not a world of objects, but precisely these other consciousnesses with their worlds, re-creates them in their authentic *unfinalizability* (which is, after all, their essence).[5]

Chapter Three
The Wreckage of Agathon

The protagonist of Gardner's second novel (1970) is, like that of his first, a professional philosopher. The setting, however, is quite different, since we find ourselves at the very beginnings of Western philosophy in ancient Sparta under the reign of Lykourgos. But this change in setting is less significant than we might expect, for the issues discussed turn out to be strikingly contemporary, or perhaps better, timeless. More important is the way these issues are dealt with. Ninth-century Greece, as portrayed by Gardner, was a hotbed of rival philosophic schools, most of which are represented by the novel's characters. The novel occupies itself directly with their contending theories and is thus more overtly philosophical and dialogical than its predecessor. The main character, the peripatetic Agathon, is an unseemly clown, quite different from the more dignified James Chandler, but this behavior, as we shall see, is consistent with Agathon's intellectual position.

Agathon's Philosophical Quest

Agathon began his philosophical work quite conventionally and seemed well launched on a promising academic career. He studied under the eminent Klinias, who rewarded his pupil's brilliance by passing on to him his precious Book, a lifelong compilation of learning and wisdom. Agathon married Tuka, daughter of a wealthy Athenian, and served as counselor to Lykourgos, the Spartan ruler. A series of tragic events exploded the young philosopher's moral and intellectual confidence, causing him to doubt himself and his quest for truth. During the Athenian war against the Megarians, Agathon killed a man in battle; drenched in his victim's blood, he was sickened by what he had done. The fact that he was led to this act by Solon's patriotic speechifying and by his wife's urgings caused Agathon to question both rhetoric and love. He experienced a second disillusioning awakening when he informed on Konon, a close friend involved in political intrigue. Konon is put to death, and Agathon, examining his conscience, could find no other explanation for his betrayal than brute impulse. This betrayal, as well as his impulsive, adulterous affairs with Iona and Thalia, shook Agathon's belief that he, or any other human, can act freely and responsibly.

Agathon made a third, shattering moral discovery when he permitted the Helots rebelling against Lykourgos to hide in the crypt that he was using to conceal his Book. The Spartans discovered the hiding place, set fire to it, and slaughtered the rebels as they tried to escape. Friends and relatives rushed to the crypt in search of their loved ones. Agathon joined them, but he was indifferent to the Helots—even to his lover Iona, who might have been among the charred victims—his only concern was for his blackened manuscript. Dorkis, Iona's husband and Agathon's friend, delivered this withering judgment to Agathon: "you care more for knowledge than for people."[1]

Agathon finds himself facing the same questions that troubled James Chandler and John Horne. Can we act freely and responsibly? Can we pursue truth and remain compassionate human beings? Agathon answers both questions in the negative, and the consequences are devastating. He generalizes from what he has discovered in his own heart and discovers that "the whole world was dead and putrefact" (102). To some degree his conclusion is justified by the greed and cruelty he finds around him, but he also meets examples of love and self-sacrifice. He does not let this deter him, however, and he pushes his generalization further, asserting universal absurdity: "THE WORLD," he declares, "IS A SHRIVELED PUMPKIN" (25).

Agathon the Buffoon

To this metaphysical and moral vacuum, Agathon has one response: buffoonery. He wanders Sparta's streets and public places, wild-eyed and filth-bespattered, farting and laughing. He mocks the city's leaders, mortifying his faithful apprentice, Peeker, and eventually landing both of them in jail. But, Agathon insists, he is serious behind his clown's mask. His antics are simply a cracked mirror that reflects and satirizes the world's fundamental foolishness.

Agathon is the first of Gardner's problematic rebels—Grendel and the Sunlight Man are two others—who irreverently mock the established order. Their scandalous behavior links them to the clowns and fools whom Bakhtin has discussed in his study of carnival.[2] The ribald jesters and tricksters of the Roman saturnalia and of the medieval feast of fools embody the spirit of carnival, which, for Bakhtin, has an important cultural function. During carnival all rules are suspended and traditional categories are reversed: commoners replace nobility, the body—particularly its reproductive functions—supplants the mind, and laughter drowns out all serious discourse. These festivities derive ultimately from ancient fertility rites, and they remain, for Bakhtin, profoundly regenerative. They explode, momentarily at least, conventions and taboos, opening culture to new perspectives, values, and energies. When this spirit enters literature, it is profoundly dialogical. Bakhtin sees Rabelais's fiction as crucial to the development of the novel because of the way the carnival spirit permeates it, opening it to the Renaissance's many divergent and conflicting languages and values. Bakhtin also tells us, however, that the clown figure—carnival's lord of misrule—undergoes important changes in the romantic and modern period. During these periods he is estranged from the forces of nature and from the common people, and he becomes increasingly the symbol of alienated, nihilistic despair.

Agathon embodies elements of both the traditional carnival clown and of his modern, alienated descendant. His sarcastic laughter is healthy when it provokes reflection and challenges unjust institutions. We should note, however, that his target is much broader than society, for he is, at bottom, a metaphysical rebel—"the absolute idea of *No*" (219). He refuses any complicity in the Helots' revolt and pushes his personal rebellion to the extreme of rejecting his friends' efforts to free him from prison. When Iona tries to liberate him, he answers angrily, "I say *No* to the universe. 'Fuck it!' saith angry Agathon. I'll have no truck with it. And so I refuse to be rescued from my cell" (220).

This rebel is a complicated and contradictory figure whose ringing jail-cell refusal suggests an intellectual confidence that he does not, in fact, possess. He reveals his deep self-doubts when, in the course of the refusal quoted above, Iona accuses him of the pomposity he has mocked in others: "I *am* pompous. It's true! O miserable, miserable beast! I *hate* myself!" (219). Agathon's buffoonery masks a deep despair and self-loathing: he capers and grimaces to mock the Spartans and the universe but also to distract himself from his own irresolution and impotence. We see the consequences of Agathon's self-consciousness in the portions of the text he narrates. His manuscript, which represents roughly half of the novel, includes direct asides to the reader and passages of comic bombast that suggest that he is clowning before us in much the same way that he clowns before the Spartan ephors. This verbal buffoonery casts doubt on the integrity of his narrative, and Iona suggests that much of it is pure invention. Peeker, his literary executor, senses, however, that at least one thing in the narrative is authentic—the drive behind it. Agathon needs at all costs to invent a face to confront the universe and to hide from us and from himself the despair and self-loathing we have described.

Agathon's voice is an important and complex component in the novel's dialogue. Agathon has looked long and hard at questions from which most of us have preferred to avert out eyes. His solution to these questions, however, is finally unsatisfactory. Thus he functions in the novel's dialogue primarily as a demonstration of the negative consequences of intellectual bad faith. This bad faith is the source of the wreckage to which the novel's title refers.

More specifically, Agathon fails because he refuses to work through, rigorously and honestly, the basic issues upon which his rebellion depends. First of all, do the gods exist, and do they control our actions? Agathon's philosophical training disposes him toward skepticism, and thus he mocks Dorkis's religious faith as "Peasant ideas. Childlike" (153). On the other hand, he experiences dreams and premonitions that suggest a world beyond the material one. He never really settles his mind on the issue and gives different answers at different moments in the novel. This failure has crucial ethical implications, for if the gods do not exist or if they have no effective control over our lives, then we must accept primary moral responsibility for our lives. This is something Agathon is unwilling to do. When called to account for his intemperate behavior, he resorts to the religious explanation he has ridiculed elsewhere: he was controlled, he says, by "an impulse from the gods" (161). Of course, this acknowledgment of the gods' power in his life does not obligate Agathon to any acts of religious piety toward them.

Agathon has a favorite metaphor—all human activity as divine flatulence—that neatly illustrates both the content and the technique of his philosophical waffling: "So it comes to this: Every event, every adventure, is a ripple in God's exhalation. Or should I say His fart?" (111; see also 217). How do we read this metaphor? Is it simply blasphemous—an irreverent mocking of the idea of divine inspiration? Or is it serious—a description of the capricious ways the gods dispose our lives? The form of the utterance—outrageous, scatological buffoonery—allows Agathon to escape without committing himself. We are surprised, amused, or perhaps scandalized, by the conceit itself, and, before we get to its implications, Agathon has slipped away amidst a fusillade of his own farts and laughter.

Competing Voices

Agathon's philosophical voice is not alone in this novel. The world through which he moves is rich in competing philosophical opinions, which his narrative reports. The novel thus places his ideas in the context of other Athenian, Spartan, and Helot thinkers. Among these is Solon, an Athenian philosopher and politician who professes a doctrine he describes as "humanism." In practice this turns out to be a tolerant political pragmatism. He repeals Draco's harsh laws and seeks to balance the contending parties in the Athenian state. He proves particularly adept at getting the lower classes to do the upper class's will. Solon, who preached the Megarian war that was the occasion of Agathon's disillusionment, has grown rich putting his intellect to the service of the state. He seems, to Agathon and to us, opportunistic and lacking in philosophical rigor. Klinias, Agathon's teacher, who argues that "ethics is like medicine, to be taken only when needed" (68), is vulnerable to the same criticism. So is Konon, a disciple of Klinias who is destroyed in the Athenian power struggle.

A philosopher who is not vulnerable to this charge is the Spartan leader Lykourgos. His philosophy is the exact opposite of Solon's tolerant but improvisitory "humanism": he is rigorously lucid about his first principles and unflinchingly consistent in working them out. The Spartans have seized some of the most fertile land in the Peloponnesus, and they fully expect that other peoples will attempt to take it from them. To prevent this they have created a powerful standing army and have emphasized military virtues over all others. They enforce military discipline, practice eugenic breeding, and exact severe punishment on all misdeeds. They also keep a subject people, the Helots, in bondage to perform all nonmilitary tasks, thus freeing the Spartans for training and combat.

This militocracy is entirely consistent with Lykourgos's philosophical vision. For the Spartan leader humans are alone in the universe, thus "a man must know himself God" (86). This moral burden is a heavy one, and the state must help shape its citizens for it: strength must be encouraged, weakness ruthlessly weeded out. Lykourgos acknowledges that the society he has fashioned is cruel and repressive, but it is perfectly suited to the brutal universe as he finds it: "imprisonment and execution are not great evils, merely mirrors, too clear for cowardly eyes, of reality as it is" (86). Agathon is initially attracted by Lykourgos's honesty and consistency, but he is eventually sickened by its brutal consequences, and so are we.

In addition to these Athenians and Spartans, there are a group of thinkers associated with the Helot rebellion. The most famous of these is Thaletes, a Kretan philosopher-poet, who has joined the Helot underground. He is captured by Lykourgos, and Agathon visits him in his prison cell. The philosophy he hears there is reminiscent of Sartrean existentialism. It is thick with phenomenological jargon, but its main themes are clear: human freedom is the highest good, and it realizes itself in resisting that which would suppress it. It is this belief that has led Thaletes to engage himself in the Helot revolt against their Spartan masters. Agathon grants that Thaletes's position makes "a kind of sense" but finally decides that he is "not particularly impressed" (188). He makes this decision less from any serious effort of working through and refuting Thaletes' arguments than from an ad hominem dismissal: he dislikes Thaletes' morbidity and mistrusts his infatuation with lost causes.

One individual who is impressed, however, is Iona. She reads all of Thaletes' writings and draws support for her rebellion from them. Thaletes' idea of human freedom as the highest good enables Iona to do what Agathon has not done. She is able, in an admittedly evil world, to discriminate between greater and lesser evils, and to act. She presents her case against Agathon's despairing dismissal of all human action and her defense of the Helots' violent rebellion:

One can no more judge the means without the end which gives it meaning than he can detach the end from the means which defines it. Murdering a Helot or suppressing a hundred members of the Opposition are two analogous acts. Murdering a Helot is an *absolute* evil—it represents the survival of an obsolete civilization, the perpetuation of a struggle of races which has to disappear! Suppressing a hundred opponents may be an outrage, but it can have meaning and a reason. It is a matter of maintaining or saving a Power which prevents *the absolute evils of bigots and despots*. (188)

Agathon does not trouble himself to consider Iona's argument; he simply dismisses it as "philosophically naive" (189). Later, when Iona persists in urging his support of the rebellion, he answers: "You plan for the future, but what you don't understand is, there *is* no future. Thaletes's words, but the voice of the universe as well. I have seen the future of the Helots, Iona. Doom. Fire and torture and decimation" (214). The argument is dishonest and contradictory. Thaletes *does* not say there is no future, only that there is no *predetermined* future: we create the future through our own free acts. After asserting that there is no future, Agathon reverses himself and says that there *is* a future and he already knows it: the Helots will be defeated. Such dishonesty and contradiction are not signs of honest dialogue but of intellectual buffoonery: playing with paradox and partial truths to confound the listener and protect the buffoon.

Iona sees past Agathon's strategy and tries to force him to confront the emptiness he has tried to hide: "Stop it, Agathon! Just for one second in your life, stop it and *look* at yourself. Those filthy clothes, that tangled hair, those wasted eyes, wasted gestures, wasted ideas! *Be* something! . . . We need your mind, your knowledge of them, your way of swaying people. . . . *Will* you come with us?" (214–15). Agathon refuses Iona's plea and offers her no further explanation. He does tell us that he was filled at this moment by "an overwhelming sense of the boundless stupidity of things" (215). If, however, we follow his actual thoughts at this time, we see that they are regrets for his personal stupidity: the frivolous way that he has discarded his wife, his mistress, his friends, and his influence. By formulating these regrets as a sense of the stupidity of *things,* he subtly shifts the focus from himself to the general order, dissolving his own culpability and absorbing it into a supposed universal absurdity.

There is another important voice in the dialogue surrounding the Helot revolt, the voice of Iona's husband, Dorkis. Dorkis is as aware as Agathon of the mutability of all things human and of the difficulty of leading a morally consistent life: "Life. Experience. It's like something alive, forever changing its shape. There's a sense in which as soon as you learn its laws it's become something else. It wreaks havoc on ethical theories" (46). Dorkis is protected from the despair into which Agathon has lapsed by a deep religious faith. All existence, no matter how incomprehensible to us, has a divine source; everything is "the breath of God" (46). Dorkis's metaphor is a variation on Agathon's scatological one, but Dorkis means it reverently, and he follows it consistently in his life. He draws great serenity and tolerance from this faith, blessing his wife's affair with Agathon and refusing to condemn his ideological opponents. His daily prayer to the gods embodies the crucial Gardnerian virtues of intellectual generosity and resilience: "Teach us to live with contradiction, and lead us, by your cunning ways, away from the dark pits of meaninglessness and despair" (228).

For all this, Dorkis is not passive. At his wife's urging, he joins the revolt and quickly becomes one of its leaders. When Helots, angered by Agathon's behavior at the massacre site, threaten to kill him, Dorkis intervenes to protect his friend. He does so at a heavy personal price, for in so doing he incriminates himself to the Spartans, who torture and eventually execute him. Despite terrible suffering, Dorkis does not betray his coconspirators, and he dies with such dignity and serenity that he earns the admiration of his torturers. Dorkis is, in many ways, the novel's most admirable character. The Spartans respect him, Peeker memorializes him, and Iona continues her fight because of him. Even Agathon acknowledges that Dorkis's "absolute and simple faith filled the room like autumn light, like a sea breeze. Even when his ideas were crazy, the man had sophrosyne, as they used to call it in the old days" (152–53). But Dorkis's ideas and actions are those of a saint—luminescent, inspiring, but perhaps inaccessible to ordinary individuals.

The Last Voice

We must consider one final voice in the novel, one of the most important in terms of the space it occupies and the perspective it provides. This is the voice of Demodokos, Agathon's philosophical apprentice, who narrates nearly half the novel. An important key to this character is the name, Peeker, that Agathon has given him. Agathon is a genuine seer: in addition to his brilliant intellect, he enjoys second sight, which enables him to glimpse things other mortals cannot. Demodokos is supposed to learn this craft from his master but realizes he will never do so—he simply lacks the gift. He is not a seer, but only a peeker. But a peeker also sees, less than the visionary, but perhaps with a sharper focus: homely truths overlooked in metaphysical flight. Peeker and Agathon thus represent a neatly balanced set of perspectives from which to narrate this story: youthful idealism versus world-weary cynicism, pedestrian common sense versus oracular brilliance, warm human concern versus egoistic self-absorption.

Peeker contributes to the novel less as a disputant defending a set of philosophical arguments than as a moral presence. All of the novel's arguments are, finally, filtered through him. He hears Agathon's fulminations, reads Solon's sermons, considers Lykourgos's sententiae, and witnesses Dorkis's saintly self-sacrifice. He provides us with a model of how to live in a world filled with contradictory ideologies and contending ideologues. He is patient: despite many frustrations, he perseveres in his pursuit of truth. He is tolerant: he even manages to identify with his Spartan captors and, to some degree, sympathize with their position. He is honest: he admits to Tuka that his beloved Agathon was fundamentally wrong. Finally, he is loving.

Agathon recognizes this love and cleverly rewards it at the end of his life. His own teacher gave him his Book; Agathon offers his pupil his daughter. By the strategy of sending him on a delivery errand after his own death, Agathon engineers Peeker's meeting with his daughter, Diana, and the two are immediately smitten. Agathon seems to understand this much at life's end: the thing a teacher must leave with his student is less a reverence for the Book—ink on parchment—than a concern for truth discovered in and through human commitment. Peeker seems already to embody that commitment.

Peeker offers a judgment of Agathon early in the novel. "The trouble is," he tells his teacher, "you can never know if you're right or wrong, and until you do you must pull your nose and scratch your ear and ask the question some other way, in a predictably futile but inescapable search for certainty" (31). Agathon vigorously disagrees, but we sense that Peeker is probably right. The comment, I think, can be applied with even greater pertinency to Gardner's novel as a whole. We sense in it a recognition that the pursuit of truth is difficult, perhaps even futile. And yet it refuses to give over; it seeks to consider issues from a multiplicity of perspectives, "to ask the question some other way," rather than to abandon the inescapable search.

Chapter Four
Grendel

The shaggy monster that we meet, capering on a cliff, at the beginning of *Grendel* (1971) seems a near relative of Agathon. Here is another rebel shaking his fists at the heavens and at the contemporary social order. Here also is another monologist, for this monster, our narrator, talks incessantly and to no other audience but himself. And yet there is an important difference: Grendel is a monologist *malgré lui*, an individual who desperately wishes for dialogue but for whom this wish is always frustrated.

Personal identity, as Bakhtin has explained, is always worked out in a social context, through dialogue with others. This is so, first of all, because the language we use to articulate our notions of ourselves is a social product: we receive it from others and learn to use it by interacting with them. Perhaps more important, we can never test, adapt, and strengthen our subjective perceptions of ourselves on our own. For this we need others who can see us as we cannot see ourselves from outside, as fixed wholes. We do not blindly accept the judgments of others, but we enter into a dialogue with them, informing them more fully about ourselves and learning from them about the world we share and their perception of our place in it. In this way, we engage in a continuing dialogue about our identity and the meaning of our experience.

It is precisely this dialogue that is denied to Grendel. He is, apparently, an evolutionary cul de sac, the only member of his species. He has a mother, but she seems locked at a more primitive level, bereft of speech. Grendel, however, is not without language, and this is, to a large degree, the source of his problem. He has attained a linguistic level of consciousness that permits him to pose questions about identity. It also enables him to comprehend the speech of humans and of a dragon. He understands them, but they cannot or will not understand him: the humans are too censorious and the dragon is too bored. Thus he is trapped in one-way communication, where others have a right to impose their meaning on him but where he has no chance for an effective response. He can neither stop his search for understanding nor drive from his consciousness the voices of these others and the philosophies they embody. He is thus trapped in an intense *interior dialogue,* in which he listens attentively to these views, considers them carefully, and argues them vociferously, if only to himself.

Grendel's Search for Understanding

Grendel's narrative, which records his struggle to understand himself and his world, proceeds in three stages. After an introductory chapter in the present, he recounts retrospectively his earlier experiences and the philosophical positions to which he has been exposed. He returns in the middle of the novel to the present and to a more detailed consideration of humans and their view of the world. The novel concludes in its final two chapters with Grendel's fatal encounter with Beowulf, the human champion.

Grendel reaches an important decision about the world's meaning in his early maturity. He finds himself trapped in an oak tree, his leg painfully wedged between two branches, under attack by an enraged bull. The physical pain is intense, but the psychological anguish is even greater. He searches the empty horizon for assistance but discovers only the hostility of the bull and the indifference of the surrounding hills. Grendel describes the awareness he achieved in this moment of pain and loneliness: "I understood that the world was nothing: a mechanical chaos of casual, brute enmity on which we stupidly impose our hopes and fears. I understood that, finally and absolutely, I alone exist. All the rest, I saw, is merely what pushes me, or what I push against, blindly—as blindly as all that is not myself pushes back. I create the whole universe, blink by blink.—An ugly god pitifully dying in a tree!"[1]

We must be careful to read this "I alone exist" in context. Grendel does not deny the literal existence of a reality outside his mind—the tree's grip on his leg is too painful for him to make that mistake. What he senses is that his existence matters to him alone. The universe he surveys from the oak tree is indifferent to him and to the meaning he must create for himself, blink by blink. The Grendel we meet here is an absurdist not a solipsist, an existentialist rather than a philosophical idealist.

These lessons about the mind and the world continue when Grendel, still trapped in the tree, first encounters humans. Although he can understand their speech, they cannot be still long enough to understand his. Instead they noisily attempt to categorize their discovery: some argue that Grendel is a tree fungus, others that he is an oak-tree spirit. When their leader endorses the latter identification, they prepare to kill Grendel, but, fortunately, he is rescued at the last moment by his mother. Grendel, however, has made an important discovery about human thinking: these "pattern makers" (27) need, at all cost, to impose *their* meanings on their surroundings, and they can be murderously efficient in enforcing those meanings. Despite their hostility to him, Grendel does not initially attack humans; in fact, he even tries to befriend a few exiled members of their community. But mainly he watches. He is impressed by the growing power of Hrothgar, their leader, but he is sickened by the cruelty, waste, and destruction that is the price of this growth.

Grendel's instruction in human culture reaches a crucial moment when he hears the Shaper, Hrothgar's court poet. He listens as this artist sings his version of the community's valorous past and its glorious future. Grendel knows this is pure invention, for he has watched the community over the years and knows the truth about the way they live. He also hears the poet tell his fellows that Grendel is their enemy, a son of Cain, cursed by God. Grendel is hurt and angered by the identity that has been unilaterally thrust upon him and from which he is granted no appeal. Despite his anger and despite the fact that he knows the truth, Grendel finds the blind singer's myth enormously seductive. Drawn by the poet's vision, Grendel tries to join the humans and staggers into their settlement crying, "Mercy! Peace!" (51). The men meet him with battleaxes, however, and he flees for his life.

Frustrated by his contacts with humans, Grendel turns to the dragon. The dragon, at least, will talk to Grendel. *To* not *with,* for genuine dialogue is not possible here. The dragon claims a superior intellect and a broader vision; the best he can manage for Grendel is a brief, patronizing lecture. He explains that humans know only a brief moment in the universe's history and that they generalize from scanty evidence. In addition, humans analyze everything, reducing the world to their categories and destroying it in the process. As a consequence, the dragon concludes, humans never truly see the big picture: "they only think they think. No total vision, total system" (64). To mask the limits of their vision, poets like the Shaper attempt a reassuring but specious synthesis, but it is "mere tripe . . . mere sleight-of-wits" (65).

The dragon attempts to share the pattern glimpsed by one who can see all time and space. He notes that all nature reveals a drive toward progressively more complex forms of order. Among the higher forms he also notes more centralized systems of organization, which can act upon the environment in a more focused way. These comments confirm what Grendel has observed and what the Shaper celebrates about humans, who exert significant control through sophisticated patterns of organization. The dragon also explains why the humans have cast Grendel as their enemy: they need a "brute existent" (73) against which they can struggle in their growth toward even higher forms of organization. But the dragon challenges the Shaper's grandiose claim that humans are the climax of all creation. He opens his historical lens for a magnification a thousand times more broad to show that this seeming pattern is only a tiny detail in a panorama that is finally chaotic. Man is no climax, merely a tiny detail in a universe constantly creating new forms, allowing some to develop briefly and then destroying them in turn. "Things come and go. . . . That's the gist of it. In a billion billion billion years, everything will have come and gone several times, in various forms" (70). The moral consequence of this vision is, for the dragon, a resigned cynicism. Since in the long term it all turns to dust, one may as well pursue one's own pleasure. For the dragon this means hoarding gold; he urges Grendel to do the same.

After visiting the dragon, Grendel is poised between conflicting visions of the world as chaos and the world as order. There is, on one hand, his own intuition of an absurd and indifferent universe and the dragon's more elaborate doctrine of meaningless time and space. In direct contrast, there is the supremely ordered human vision celebrated by the Shaper: an illustrious historical progress climaxing in the reign of Hrothgar, which is now imposing itself on the landscape in the system of roads radiating out from his palace.

Shortly thereafter, Grendel makes his first raid on the human settlement and, in so doing, discovers his identity:

I was transformed. I was a new focus for the clutter of space I stood in: if the world had once imploded on the tree where I waited, trapped and full of pain, it now blasted outward, away from me, screeching terror. . . . I had *become* something, as if born again. I had hung between possibilities before, between the cold truths I knew and the heart-sucking conjuring tricks of the Shaper; now that was passed: I was Grendel, Ruiner of Meadhalls, Wrecker of Kings. (80)

Despite this initial exhilaration, Grendel is almost immediately dissatisfied with this identity. By his seeming act of self-creation, Grendel has, in fact, accepted and reinforced the signification that the Shaper earlier assigned him. This meaning admirably serves human needs: he is the Enemy, the brute against which humans define themselves and by means of which they justify their claims of superiority. But it does little for Grendel: he is trapped in a static, negative identity that denies him any chance for growth and that ensures his status as a permanent outsider. Paradoxically, Grendel, in the very act of opposing the human community, affirms their power over him. He does this continually when he uses human language to articulate his consciousness. Thus he imitates the Shaper's alliterations and kennings in his own angry soliloquies, and he discovers to his disgust that, when he wants to curse humans, he must use human profanities to do so.

Grendel's Voices

Grendel's confusion is emotional as well as linguistic, and the narrative's central chapters dramatize his conflicting feelings about human culture. All of his instincts and all that he has seen contradict the Shaper's vision, and yet when Grendel hears the poet strike his harp or when he watches Wealtheow, Hrothgar's beautiful queen, he feels magnetically drawn. He tries to work through these contradictory emotions in two "cuts" from a "Time-Space cross-section" that he narrates in chapters 7 and 8.

These narratives are artistic creations. More than anywhere else in his narrative, Grendel deliberately exploits the techniques of epic, dramatic, lyric, and novelistic art to tell his story. Some of what he tells is based on direct observation, but much of it is the inner life—the secret thoughts, hopes, and fears—of the characters. Grendel can have no direct access to these materials; they are artistic imaginings, the product of his sympathetic identification with humans. Grendel accomplishes something that no one else in the narrative does and something that is essential to dialogical fiction and, indeed, to civilized life: he manages to see the world through his ideological opponents' eyes, to entertain seriously their worldview and even to accept it for the duration of these episodes.

Grendel devotes the first of these cuts to Wealtheow and to the human values of love, sacrifice, and forgiveness embodied by Hrothgar's queen. But balance is all, and Grendel follows this with another episode, "Cut B," devoted to Hrothulf. This story of Hrothgar's nephew cold-bloodedly plotting his uncle's overthrow illustrates the egoism, pride, and violence that Grendel has also seen among the humans. Thus Grendel, in these imaginative creations, as in his behavior, hangs "balanced, a creature of two minds" (110), in his feelings about human culture.

As we see in the narrative skill and verbal ingenuity of his story, Grendel is a literary artist. He can use language to analyze, to criticize, to mock, and to imagine, but he is not allowed to use it to communicate. Grendel cannot use his language to share, and thus to confirm or modify, his view of the world. "Why," he asks, "can't I have someone to talk to?" (53). He could have someone, for humans *can* understand him if they make the effort, as Grendel proves when he forces Unferth to listen; it is simply that they are too intent on using Grendel for their own purposes to do so.

Denied a community, Grendel has only his own voices from which to construct his dialogue. These include not only the voices he has heard and internalized—those of the Shaper and the dragon—but a multiplicity of personal voices. Indeed, one of his most serious disabilities is the fact that he has no single, stable personal voice with which to respond to the voices of others. His personality and his consciousness is split and divided against itself, and we see the consequences of this in the very texture of his narration. Consider, for example, the conflicting attitudes, styles, and tones present in one of the novel's first paragraphs:

(It was just here . . . that . . . I tore off sly old Athelgard's head. Here, where the startling tiny jaws of crocuses snap at the late-winter sun like the heads of baby watersnakes, here I killed the old woman with the irongray hair. She tasted of urine and spleen, which made me spit. Sweet mulch for yellow blooms. Such are the tiresome memories of a shadow-shooter, earth-rim-roamer, walker of the world's weird wall.) "Waaah!" I cry, with another quick, nasty face at the sky, mournfully observing the way it is, bitterly remembering the way it was, and idiotically casting tomorrow's nets. "Aargh! Yaww!" I reel, smash trees. Disfigured son of lunatics. The big-boled oaks gaze down at me yellow with morning, beneath complexity. "No offense," I say, with a terrible sycophantish smile, and tip an imaginary hat. (7)

Listen to the stunning range of voices in this passage: we hear a brutal killer and a sensitive crocus lover, a master of epic alliteration and a bawling crybaby, a tree-smashing rebel and a grinning sycophant. Lacking an interlocutor, Grendel is forced to perform all of the parts in his dialogue himself. He is constantly anticipating and objecting internally; thus the voice that brashly challenges the heavens suddenly expresses doubts, then apologizes, and finally mocks itself. Under such conditions, Grendel's metaphysical questioning can quickly turn to anguished verbal play: "I observe myself observing what I observe. It startles me. 'Then I am not that which observes!' I am *lack*. *Alack!*" (29). Grendel's language, his only resource, becomes for him a frustrating "web of words, pale walls of dreams" (8). Rather than putting him in contact with others, it further isolates him; instead of settling his doubts, it multiplies them. Grendel's internal dialogue threatens to become an internal cacophony.

Grendel's internal confusion affects his behavior, and he often gives over to the desperate clowning we saw above. Like Agathon, Grendel is a buffoon, but there are differences. Agathon has a community; his buffoonery is frequently playful, and he mocks the society he rejects. Grendel is alone; his buffoonery has a darker tone, and he aims it at himself. Agathon wants to avoid confronting his internal contradictions and uses his clowning to distract himself. Grendel, in contrast, is all too aware of his contradictions and uses his buffoonery to punish himself for not being able to resolve them.

The Fatal Encounter with Beowulf

Grendel's fatal confrontation with Beowulf will end his frustrated quest and his life. The hero's arrival excites Grendel, and he comes almost by appointment to the hall where Beowulf waits. From out of the darkness, Beowulf seizes him in a painful grip, and Grendel finds himself "grotesquely shaking hands" with the man he calls his "dear long-lost brother, kinsman-thane" (168–69). The combatants are, from the human perspective, descendants of brothers, but this consanguinity, rather than joining them, opposes them in the age-old enmity of Abel and Cain. Grendel, however, seems to hint at something more in these words: Beowulf finally might have been the one who could have understood him. But this is not the age of dialogue, and they will act to define one another, not in reasoned discourse, but in bloody combat.

With Grendel safely locked in his grip, Beowulf instructs him in his own view of the world. His lessons are brief, and, on many points, they repeat what Grendel has already sensed or what he has heard from the dragon. Here is what Beowulf tells Grendel:

As you see it it is, while the seeing lasts, dark nightmare-history, time-as-coffin; but where the water was rigid there will be fish, and men will survive on their flesh till spring. It's coming, my brother. Believe it or not. Though you murder the world, turn plains to stone, transmogrify life into I and it, strong searching roots will crack your cave and rain will cleanse it: The world will burn green, sperm build again. My promise. Time is the mind, the hand that makes (fingers on harpstrings, hero-swords, the acts, the eyes of queens). By that I kill you. (170)

Beowulf, like the dragon, concedes that, from Grendel's perspective, the world may seem a senseless nightmare. Nonetheless, there is a pattern. For Beowulf, as for the dragon, this pattern includes both birth and decay, but where the dragon chose to emphasize decay, Beowulf emphasizes the rebirth that always follows it. He reminds Grendel that, although he may try to disassociate himself and ignore these regenerative forces, they will make themselves felt in the the annual renewal of nature, as well as in the harper's song, the queen's smiling eyes, and the hero's act of courage.

Beowulf next reminds his adversary of what Grendel surmised in the oak tree—that we impose meaning on the world: "You make the world by whispers, second by second. . . . Whether you make it a grave or a garden of roses is not the point" (171). Grendel offers no comment, but Beowulf does not care; his way is not persuasion—rough compulsion will do as well. He smashes Grendel's head against the wall: "Feel the wall: is it not hard? . . . Observe the hardness, write it down in careful runes. Now sing of walls!" (171). If the point of this head bashing is to prove to Grendel that an external reality exists, Beowulf's lesson is pointless, since Grendel has never been a solipsist. The purpose of Grendel's search—the visit to the dragon, the spying on humans—has been to understand reality not to deny it. It seems, then, that Beowulf speaks, not of walls in general, but of the specific walls in this context, the walls of Hrothgar's banqueting hall. Grendel must submit to these symbols of human power as the other lords have had to submit to Hrothgar.

Grendel sings, but he, in fact, concedes little. Here is his song:

> The wall will fall to the wind as the
> windy hill
> will fall, and all things thought in
> former times:
> Nothing made remains, nor man remembers.
> And these towns shall be called the
> shining towns! (172)

The first sentence of Grendel's poem says nothing more than what the dragon has already said—all things pass. The final sentence concedes, however, that the human achievement will survive, luminous in the memory of other humans. Privately, Grendel concedes even less: Beowulf, he whispers, is mad, and the world is mere accident.

We find that Grendel has come full circle; the spot to which Beowulf has dragged him reminds us of the rocky cliff where we first met him, his middle finger raised in defiance to the heavens. He cries out for his mother and finds himself, as in the traumatic episode in the tree, once again surrounded by an uncomprehending, indifferent universe. Bleeding from his wounds, Grendel moves, as if magnetically propelled, to the cliff's edge. He has felt the pull of the abyss before, and this time he accedes, jumping to his death. His final words repeat his claim that everything, his death included, is the result of brute chance. They are also a curse that we may know the same fate: "Poor Grendel's had an accident. . . . *So may you all*" (174).

Beowulf conquers Grendel, but it is difficult to see this killing as a moral victory. Grendel, it is true, is a raider and a killer, but so are Hrothgar and his thanes; the principal difference seems to be that Hrothgar allows his acts to be glorified in song while Grendel freely admits the nature of his deeds. Indeed, Grendel, the putative monster, seems, in many ways, more honest, sensitive, and reflective than his human adversaries. One of the crucial questions his narrative raises is, in fact, what is a monster? For Red Horse, Hrothulf's tutor, it is his fellow humans: their systems of organization—subjugating other humans, reducing nature—are "*monstrously* evil" (120).

Still, we cannot simply reverse the traditional judgments and turn Grendel into a sentimental victim. He is too self-aware and tough minded to make such a claim for himself. He is also too genuinely attracted to certain humans to cast them as melodramatic villains. Grendel's final confrontation with Beowulf does little to resolve the questions his narrative has posed. Beowulf states his own position in a perfunctory manner and makes no effort to understand or persuade Grendel. Grendel, for his part, goes to his death insisting that the world is brutal, indifferent, and absurd. Thus, at Grendel's death, the issues raised in his internal dialogue remain open, and we find ourselves, like Grendel, poised between conflicting visions of order and disorder.

Grendel as Metafiction

But there is another level of dialogue in this book. In addition to the internal debate within Grendel's consciousness, there is a level of discourse of which he is totally ignorant: a dialogue between the book and the literary tradition of which it is part. Grendel's story derives from and comments upon *Beowulf,* the epic that is conventionally regarded as the beginning point for the literature of the English-speaking world. Grendel cannot know this, but all literate modern readers do, and this knowledge bears on their experience of this novel. Gardner's novel then is, at this level, a metafiction, a fiction that takes as its subject the fact that it is a work of literary art. Gardner, in his moralistic voice, has criticized such fiction, preferring more authentically "moral" narratives that occupy themselves exclusively with the real world. But this art-reality dichotomy is difficult to apply in practice, since art is *part* of reality and often decisively influences our understanding of it. Indeed, this is precisely Grendel's problem: he finds himself simultaneously drawn and repulsed by the Shaper's epic vision, and this ambivalence is crucial to his inner confusion.

Gardner's novel, then, continues this consideration of the epic vision on the metafictional level. It borrows characters and events from the famous epic, but in so doing it changes and comments upon them. Beowulf, the epic's main figure, for instance, does not appear until the novel's penultimate chapter. The novel, moreover, recounts only the first of his three famous victories, and so his stature is necessarily diminished. If the novel reduces Beowulf's importance, it dramatically increases the attention given to several of the epic's minor characters. Hrothulf, for instance, makes only a brief appearance in the epic. Scandinavian sources, however, tell us that, upon Hrothgar's death,

Hrothulf usurped the throne and killed the legitimate heir. The novel exploits this material and uses it in Grendel's "Cut B" on Hrothulf. As a consequence we are made aware of the brutality, cynicism, and naked ambition that were part of the epic world.

Unferth's role, a minor one in the original epic, is also significantly expanded in the novel. During one of Grendel's raids, Unferth boasts of his heroic stature and challenges Grendel to combat. Grendel confounds the "hero" by refusing to play the part Unferth has scripted for him; instead he humiliates Unferth by pelting him with apples. Later, Unferth, obsessed by his loss of face, makes his way to Grendel's lair, half hoping that Grendel will kill him and expunge his humiliation. Again Grendel refuses to play the role in which Unferth has cast him; Unferth, near tears, spouts increasingly contradictory and inappropriate heroic clichés and even threatens suicide. Grendel waits him out and finally deposits him, sleeping like a child, at Hrothgar's hall. Unferth never quite recovers and sinks into despondency, reviving only to question Beowulf in a churlish manner. The expanded character of Unferth shows us that the problem with the monological epic vision is that it posits a morally unambiguous world, a world in which life's most important questions can be settled by reference to a simple code. Unfortunately for Unferth, the world that Grendel—and the modern reader—inhabits does not respond to prepackaged solutions. Unferth, unprepared, cannot adapt and collapses pathetically.

In addition to borrowing characters and events, the novel takes passages from the epic, translates them, and inserts them into the novel. For example, Grendel hears the Shaper justify the human claims to superiority over Grendel by reciting the lines of the epic that call Grendel a son of the murderer Cain; this occurs, however, just after Grendel steps over a man murdered by *humans*. Several nights later when he hears the poet piously sing the lines forbidding the taking of human life, Grendel, who has seen a good deal of human slaughter, whispers an emphatic "Bullshit!" (54). In this way, the novel places passages from the epic into contexts that challenge them.

Other passages, however, occur in situations that have a different effect. The conversations between Beowulf and the coast guard and between Beowulf and Unferth in the novel are almost verbatim translations from the epic. These scenes show Beowulf's steely self-confidence and his verbal skill. Grendel's awestruck reaction confirms the epic's portrait of Beowulf as a resourceful, charismatic hero. Elsewhere, Grendel is moved by the beauty of the poet's song and the

nobility of Wealthoew's sacrifice. The grudging admiration of the epic
society's traditional enemy confirms the power of its worldview. Thus,
in this novel, the medieval and the modern, the epic and the existen-
tial, exist side by side. What can be said about the function of this
ideological coexistence?

The first thing to note, it seems to me, is the way the two views
comment upon and criticize one another. Grendel's point of view
makes us aware of the epic vision's dark side—the violence and greed
it often masked. The surviving epic elements in the novel make us
aware, by contrast, of the poverty—the loneliness and self-absorption—of the modern absurdist perspective. Setting the two sets of values side by side, then, results in a dialogue between them. This is
particularly remarkable, for dialogue of this kind was, as Bakhtin has
shown, what the epic world lacked.

Besides *Beowulf*, Gardner's novel alludes to a wide range of other
literary sources. The most important of these is William Blake, whose
"The Mental Traveller" provides the novel's epigraph:

> And if the Babe is born a Boy
> He's given to a Woman Old,
> Who nails him down upon a rock,
> Catches his shrieks in cups of gold.

Blake's lines echo Grendel's situation—his cave, his mother, and, especially, his suffering. Placed here they dispose us to view the monster
compassionately. There are numerous other, less obvious echoes of
Blake, as well as of Chaucer, Milton, Shelley, Arnold, Thomas Kinsella, and even Kurt Vonnegut.[2] The first thing that these literary
allusions do, once they are recognized, is to pull the novel's verbal
surface into focus, to remind us that it too is a "web of words," an
artificial order imposed by an artist. It also reminds us that this particular order is part of the larger order of our literary tradition. The
number of these references and their heterogeneity result in a range of
stylistic voices that, at the metafictional level, are the counterpart of
the multiple ideological voices encountered in Grendel's narrative.
They suggest that Grendel's divided consciousness is a microcosm of
our heterogeneous and divergent culture.

In addition to the pattern of literary allusions, there is another system of references at the metafictional level—references to cycles. The
novel's epigraph suggests one of these, since those who have read

Blake's poem will know that the Babe will suffer, die, and be replaced by another Babe, who will repeat the cycle. The cycles can also be seen in the novel's structure, for it is a narrative that begins and ends on a cliff and a novel whose twelve chapters cover the twelve months of the twelfth year of Grendel's rebellion. The novel's most important reference to cycles, however, is its astrological patterning. Each of the novel's twelve chapters contains one or more references to one of the zodiac's signs, beginning with Aries in the spring and continuing to Pisces in the winter.[3] The elaborate circularity of the novel's design seems to deny Grendel's absurdist vision of a world without significant pattern and to confirm Beowulf's regenerative vision of a world constantly renewing itself.

It is important to note, however, that this pattern is imposed from outside the narrative. The astrological allusions have not been placed there by Grendel, the narrator, for he is ignorant of human science and specifically rejects looking to the stars for "meaningful patterns that do not exist" (11). These references have, moreover, only an incidental relationship to the narrative itself. They are a layer of deliberate literary patterning imposed by the author, and I think we are meant to recognize them as such. Taken with the self-conscious literary references, they remind us once again that what we are considering is not a piece of the world but a work of literary art.

The novel, then, continues, at the metafictional level, the dialogue on order and chaos begun within the narrative. The Shaper outside the narrative—John Gardner—resembles the Shaper inside the narrative in that he gives us an intensely ordered vision of the world. This modern poet, however, does something that his medieval counterpart did not do: he deliberately and self-consciously calls our attention to the artificiality of his structuring patterns. In so doing, he reminds us that the design we encounter in his story is one he has imposed, not one he has discovered in the world itself. It is a distinction worth keeping in mind, for wars, witch hunts, and pogroms have been caused by those who have forgotten it. Gardner is aware of this danger: his narrative reminds us that our patterns, to contain, must also exclude, and it shows us the monster-making consequences of such exclusion.

This novel, then, allows us to join the Shaper in his celebration of epic order. But, before it permits us to join the circle around the campfire, it demands that we first step over the bloody corpse of Grendel.

Chapter Five
The Sunlight Dialogues

Grendel's struggle is that of the individual versus the group, the private need to assert one's identity against the community's need to protect order. In *The Sunlight Dialogues* (1972) Gardner returns to this problem and treats it in a modern setting. The time is the 1960s, the place rural America. The Judeo-Christian worldview, which Hrothgar and his Shaper labored to install over a thousand years ago, seems now to be decaying, and with it the moral consensus it so long sustained. In the absence of this consensus, do the requirements of order simply become naked power relationships—a dominant majority imposing its values on a weaker minority? The question is political in its most immediate implications, but its roots, Gardner would insist, are in our metaphysical, religious, and moral confusion.

Gardner, discussing this novel, has described the competing claims of the community and the individual: "I think you have to keep your merely social values to some extent. They give identity. Security. But you must recognize that they're not universally shared . . . and that, in the realm of public values, we have to compromise; we have to try to dismiss what our own fraction of the culture calls 'bad manners' and ask only for humane goodness." He immediately recognizes, however, that such compromises can, if pushed far enough, lead to an impotent relativism: "If we abandon all we've come from, what we get is— nothing. We poison our emotions."[1] But how, in this changed environment, do we arrive at universal values, how do we discover a shared definition of "humane goodness"? The solution, Gardner suggests, may emerge from developing "a powerful sense of empathy for other people through particular relationships with other people. In doing that you get a clear sense of what the universal values are without abandoning your own personal supports, the rituals that differently express the universal."[2]

The Central Conflict: Tag Hodge and Fred Clumly

The answer, in short, is dialogue: the search for moral consensus through the generous and sympathetic consideration of opposed per-

42

spectives. Dialogue understood in this sense is the subject of this novel. The title suggests as much, but we must be careful not to construe this title too narrowly, for, if we take it as referring exclusively to the four "dialogues" directed by Tag Hodge—the self-proclaimed Sunlight Man—to Fred Clumly, the book might better be named *The Twilight Monologues*. Twilight because the novel is suffused with the crepuscular glow of a declining moral order and because Tag Hodge's opaque sermons bring as much obscurity as light to our understanding of this decline. Monologues because Tag's sermons are pure one-man performances: Clumly is reduced to the silent—and sometimes somnolent—target of Tag's attacks.

But seen more broadly the novel is indeed dialogical: the central problem of private versus public values—anarchy versus order—is dramatized in many different characters. The list published at the front of the book identifies more than seventy characters, and this list is only partial. We enter the minds of more than a dozen of these characters at one point or another in the narrative. If anything the novel is too diverse, and critics have attacked its lengthy digressions on minor characters. The novel's unseemly diversity is an implicit denunciation of Tag's monological style, which refuses to entertain any perspective but its own: Gardner's discourse reaches out generously to incorporate seemingly marginal points of view. Despite the formal sprawl that results, the central opposition of Tag Hodge and Fred Clumly provides a focus for the narrative's many elements. The echoes of this confrontation are heard in the novel's other lives, drawing them together dramatically and thematically.

The novel takes place in and around Batavia, New York, an area long under the influence of the Hodge family. The Honorable Arthur Hodge, Sr., the family patriarch and a nearly mythic figure in the community, served as the area's congressman during a period when democracy was at its peak. A unique civic harmony existed in the region because of the intelligent tolerance practiced by leaders like Hodge, who fairly heard and adjudicated competing claims while staunchly protecting shared values. Already on the eve of World War II, the congressman could see this civil harmony and moral consensus weakening; in August 1966, when this novel opens, it has fairly disappeared.

The changed moral climate can be sensed in the decline of the Hodge family, as seen in the story of the congressman's youngest son, Taggert. Tag, more than any of his brothers, seemed destined to claim his father's place as a community leader. After returning from the war a hero, graduating from law school and marrying the daughter of a prominent figure, he seemed well on his way toward such a career. But already in his youth Tag's brilliance rested on a weak moral foundation. He bested his older brother Ben in a VFW speech contest by plagiarizing from a library book. Put to the test in adulthood, this moral foundation cracked. When his wife, Kathleen, was stricken with mental illness, Tag embezzled money to pay for her care. He was disbarred when the fraud was discovered and disfigured when his wife set fire to their home. He fled the community, his career and his personal life in ruins. Tag blames Clive Paxton, his wealthy, autocratic father-in-law, who refused to help his daughter, thus forcing Tag to act illegally. Tag gradually realizes, however, that he must share the blame, for he might have better helped his wife had he acted less impulsively.

Now, sixteen years after his disappearance, Tag returns to Batavia. He secretly visits his father-in-law, apparently planning to make peace. But something goes wrong, and Paxton is found dead. Tag's memory of the event is blocked, but it partially returns late in the novel: apparently Tag tried to strangle Paxton, triggering a fatal heart attack. The inflexible, self-righteous Paxton very likely refused Tag's overtures, insulting him and inciting the attack. Tag's returning memories include a fascinating detail—the image of Paxton blends with that of his father, suggesting that Tag's anger extends beyond Paxton to the family and community order that Tag's father symbolizes.

Tag is once again an outlaw in his home community. His frustrated attempt at reconciliation has reinforced what he had learned through his earlier tragedies: the world is brutal and unfair. Here is a glimpse of his absurdist vision: "The universe is a great machine gun, and all things physical are riddled sooner or later with bleeding holes. You're bombarded by atoms, colors, smells, textures; torn apart by ancient ideas, appeals for compassion." For Tag, all attempts to structure this confusion are futile: "you force your riddled world into order, but it collapses, riddled as fast as you build, and you build it all over again. You put up bird-houses and cities, for instance, but cats eat the birds and cyclones eat the cities, and nothing is left but the fruitless searching, which is otherwise called the soul."[3] Reacting to this dispiriting vision, Tag becomes a metaphysical rebel, a "skylight smasher" (54) shaking his fist at the universe. He focuses his rebellion by singling out Police Chief Fred Clumly, protector of the local order.

Tag gets himself arrested for a misdemeanor, then leads a jailbreak that eventually results in several murders. While at large he arranges meetings with Clumly to argue his opposition to all that Clumly represents. In these "dialogues" Tag refers frequently to the ancient Babylonians, who, according to Tag, developed methods of dealing with the fundamental chaos, which were superior to the methods developed by the Jews and the Greeks. Hebrew and classic civilization tried to pass beyond the material world to understand spiritual reality. The Babylonians, in contrast, believed that the material and spiritual were radically separate and that the the spiritual was totally unknowable. They accepted this state of affairs by being thoroughgoing materialists, reverencing "the essential holiness of matter" (318) and delighting in the life of the senses. They were free of the guilt that haunts Judeo-Christian culture, and they happily followed their sensual appetites wherever they might lead.

The Babylonians were also free of the Greek need to understand ultimate causes. They used divination and intuition to sense the general flow of things and to put themselves in that flow. Such an intuitive approach values individual preference over the tradition of law championed by Clumly. "There are no laws," Tag argues, "only the laws of man, which are easily beaten, and the laws which you make up for yourself, which may be obeyed, once they're made up, but only then" (520–21). Beneath this acceptance of the senses and intuition lies a dark pessimism. The Babylonians understood that, finally, death conquers all, and they embodied this despairing vision in their literature and architecture. Tag has embraced this vision and applies it in predicting our culture's future: "Hell's jaws will yawn and the cities will sink, and there will not be a trace" (632). To punctuate this apocalyptic prediction, Tag sends the Hodge ancestral mansion up in flames.

I realize that in summarizing Tag's position I have changed it, for the summary suggests a clarity, logic, and coherence that Tag's sermons lack. Indeed, the ideals of logic and coherence, which are crucial to traditional notions of discourse, seem to be among the prime targets of Tag's attack. As he develops his ideas, he deliberately sabotages the elements that might make them convincing. He builds his case with material drawn from two sources: archaeology and personal anecdote. The conjunction of such disparate elements—objective social science and personal confession—is, in itself, a challenge to normal philosophical and cultural analysis, but Tag pushes the challenge much further, undercutting each of these elements individually. In the archaeological portions he leaps from slight evidence to broad generalizations in a way that would shock a genuine scholar. In the

autobiographical portion he announces after the first anecdote that it
was a lie and then goes on to an even less credible incident. Throughout all portions he careens recklessly from topic to topic, scattering
arcane and nonsensical allusions, alternately boring and bewildering
his listener.

Tag accompanies these disquisitions with elaborate stage illusions.
These stagings allow him to mock the centers of the authority he attacks: the police station, the church, the cemetery, and finally the
Hodge mansion. Tag seems also to deliberately mock himself and the
seriousness of his topics, ascending a Christian pulpit to expound his
religious views and popping out of a tomb to lecture on death. He does
not use the tricks to convince us that he truly possesses occult powers;
quite the contrary, their theatricality seem to advertise the fact that
the tricks are elaborate and convincing stage illusions and that their
perpetrator is simply a talented stage performer.

This delight in performance reminds us of Agathon and provides the
key to understanding Tag Hodge. Like Agathon, Tag began a promising career but became deeply disillusioned when he discovered that
the world is not as he supposed. A different individual might have
responded to this recognition by trying to understand the world in its
own terms or by pledging solidarity with others who suffer. Tag does
neither; he makes no attempt at serious philosophical or social analysis,
and he proves as indifferent to the men he releases from jail as Agathon
was to the Helots. Tag and Agathon's deepest concern is neither with
the world nor with others but with themselves. They become star per-
formers in a theater of the self, flaunting and relishing their primal
disappointment. They transform their lives into self-consuming arti-
facts, buffoonish personas that punish others—and, ironically, themselves—for the fact that the world has not been as they would wish it.
Near the end Tag seems to reach out for community. But it all ends in
death, as it did for Agathon, when Tag finds the policeman's bullet for
which he seems to have been searching.

Tag selects as the audience and target of his critique Fred Clumly, a
man he characterizes as "the coldly reasonable unreason of officialdom"
(305). Tag will discover that Clumly is a good deal more sensitive than
he expects, but he is not wrong in seeing Clumly as his opposite. The
contrast begins with their origins. Clumly, the son of an alcoholic
plumber, both respects and resents the privileged Hodge family. He
has had his own personal tragedies, although these are less dramatic
than those suffered by Tag. A strange disease has left him entirely

without hair, and his wife has gone completely blind during their marriage. These misfortunes, however, have deepened Clumly rather than making him a rebel. Despite the misfortune he has seen, Clumly believes in an orderly universe and in the capacity for humans to act morally. Thus he sets high professional standards for himself: "I'm responsible for this town. . . . It's like a king. I don't mean I'm comparing myself to a king, you understand, but it's *like* a king. If a king's laws get tangled up and his knights all fail him, he's got to do the job himself. They're *his* people. He's responsible" (378).

Earlier in his career, this moral seriousness had made Clumly rigid and self-righteous, and it is memories of this younger Clumly that cause Tag to select him as his target. Traces of this rigidity survive, as we see when Clumly upbraids a subordinate for not arresting a prostitute, but the years have taught him tolerance and greater maturity. This maturity and tolerance will be tested and will grow significantly during the course of his meetings with the Sunlight Man, and he will prove himself more capable of true human understanding than is Tag.

We see the differences between Tag and Clumly in their respective analyses of the typical policeman. Tag has written an article, "Policework and Alienation," which argues that the law officer must inevitably become alienated from other humans. Clumly reads the essay and disagrees. He cannot draw on the sociological, psychological, and philosophical tools that Tag uses, but he has firsthand experience and a remarkable sensitivity. We then get a remarkably subtle appreciation of Clumly's police officer colleagues—their thoughts and desires—narrated from Clumly's point of view. But the greatest indication of his capacity for sympathetic understanding is his relationship with Tag. The pursuit of "the *whole* truth" (225) about Tag—the reasons Tag feels and acts as he does—totally absorbs Clumly, so much so that it threatens his job. His growth as a human being through this search becomes the novel's central theme and its principal answer to Tag's despairing nihilism.

Late in the novel, Clumly hears a psychiatrist explain Jung's metaphor of the sun: the human psyche rises from darkness in childhood, ascends in self-awareness in adulthood, and sinks again into darkness in old age. Tag would probably construe the figure as another instance of absurdity: the inevitable decay of all that we achieve in life. Clumly finds a more positive meaning. The individual declines, it is true, but not before winning something valuable for the culture. He considers in this context the role of the aged in traditional cultures:

The old people were the keepers of the law, the guardians of the mysteries: it was not a case of mere sinking into the unconsciousness of childhood, it was a further progress, a final stage in the sun's long ride into darkness, and in that final stage the sun carried all it had known before, all its intellect and activity, but now surpassed mere intellect and activity, surpassed mere propagation, mere earning, mere things of nature, and rose to the things of culture, to civilization. (605)

Clumly feels, in the shortness of his breath and in the stiffness of his joints, the waning of his physical strength. At the same time, paradoxically, he feels that his moral understanding is growing. Clumly attempts in the novel's final moments to share the fruit of this growth with his community, and in so doing becomes the novel's true Sunlight Man. The occasion is a talk on "Law and Order," scheduled many weeks earlier, before the Dairyman's League. We can imagine the litany of familiar clichés that a younger Clumly might have produced under this rubric, but the mature Clumly, learning of Tag's death as he ascends the podium, offers a eulogy for his slain adversary.

He also offers his reflections on the issues raised in Tag's sermons and, in so doing, transforms those sermons into the occasion for a true dialogue. Form was part of the content for Tag, and so it is here for Clumly; but Clumly's style is very different from Tag's. Tag was indifferent—perhaps even contemptuous—of his less-educated listener, piling on recondite allusions and careening wildly from topic to topic. Clumly speaks clearly and respectfully to his assembled neighbors: "good people, all of you, the kind of people that can sympathize with whoever gives them a fair chance" (668). He confronts them honestly, his eyes filling with tears, baring his deepest doubts as well as his still vital faith.

His first topic is Tag's theme—injustice. He freely admits that the world is often unjust and absurd, a fact amply illustrated by Tag's accidental death at the moment of his surrender. Clumly also speaks of order, and here he invokes our experience at the funeral of a just man. He has in mind the graveside ceremony for Mickey Salvador, whose death in many ways resembles Tag's. Within two weeks of each other, both men were shot with police revolvers and bled to death on the same police station floor. Mickey, killed accidentally in a jailbreak, died a death as pointless as Tag's. As with the sun metaphor, Clumly opens the perspective to look at this life in the social context, for it is only there that the order can be glimpsed: thus the importance of the funeral—the community's moment to reflect on the life that has ended. The people at Mickey's graveside saw in his short career a life that affirmed the values of decency, love, and service. In the pattern of a human life that can only be glimpsed at its end, they found strength for their own continuing struggle: "all the dignity of Mickey Salvador's life was there. . . . At last, whatever tensions, uncertainties, joys and sorrows warred in the heart, law and order were restored, and there was peace" (380).

Tag is driven to his nihilistic perspective by his total, narcissistic focus on his own tragedy: he fails to look past himself to his community and to see that the community has the power to transform tragedy by learning from it. Clumly wants to make sure this happens with Tag's death. The lesson here is to eliminate the injustices and avoid the indifference that froze Tag out:

We all live in the hope and faith that, although there may still be some faults in our society . . . we're trying to get better, doing our level best in that direction. It's a little like the Einstein universe . . . which is reaching outwards and outwards at terrific speed, and the danger is . . . it can get cold. Turn ice . . . we mustn't let that happen . . . we must all be vigilant against growing indifferent to people less fortunate. (670)

Clumly offers no assurance that such vigilance will save us, but it is all we have. He ends his sermon with a fervent prayer for generosity, compassion, and tolerance: "Blessed are the meek, by which I mean all of us, including the Sunlight Man. . . . God be kind to all Good Samaritans and also bad ones. For of such is the Kingdom of Heaven" (672). His listeners initially remain silent; then, as if to signal they have understood and that they have discovered a shared notion of humane goodness, they rise in a powerful, spontaneous ovation.

Echoes of the Central Conflict

The interaction between Tag Hodge and Fred Clumly is the novel's central narrative line, and the conflicts it dramatizes—individual versus collective values, self-absorption versus service to others, anarchy versus order—echo throughout the novel. They are seen in the contrast between Millie Hodge and her son Luke, both of whom are held prisoner by Tag. Millie sees herself as Tag's rebel ally, but they never act in concert, nor can they, since their rebellions spring from different

sources. Tag's revolt is a metaphysical rebellion against an absurd, unjust world, but Millie's is a personal vendetta against the Hodge family. She cannot forget the humiliation of growing up poor in the
shadow of the wealthy and powerful Hodges. She uses marriage to join
them, and when the family fails to live up to her expectations, she
punishes her husband with open adultery. Her revolt is less philosophical than Tag's, but it is, in many ways, more honest. She is ruthlessly
candid about herself and freely acknowledges her personal selfishness
and her indifference to others.

Luke inherits his mother's clarity of sight, but not her egoism. He
has suffered through his parents' disastrous marriage, and we suspect
that these traumas are the root of the painful migraines he suffers. His
suffering has made him sharp-tongued but not vindictive, and he manages to understand and sympathize with both his parents. Luke realizes
that this capacity to understand those with whom one disagrees was
central to the order created by his grandfather: "The Old Man knew
the secret, that was all. He knew how to see into all of them, feel out
their hearts inside his own, love them and hate them and forgive them:
he understood that nothing devoutly believed is mere error, though it
may be only half-truth, and so he could give them what they needed"
(640). Luke also understands that his grandfather's understanding did
not prevent him from making a choice and acting on it: "He got up
outside of himself to where he could act as though he himself, his own
life, were irrelevant" (641). Luke follows his grandfather and acts selflessly, giving his own life in an attempt to stop Tag's destructive program. Although Tag survives the car wreck that Luke engineers, the
narrator informs us that, in the final analysis, it was "Luke's crash that
killed him" (642). Tag surrenders shortly after the crash, perhaps
shocked into this action by Luke's sacrifice.

Luke's father Will and his brother Will Jr. both try to act in the
Hodge tradition of defending order, but neither is particularly effective. They are men of good will, but lack the congressman's energy
and vision. Will Sr. ruefully admits this deficiency in himself and so
confines himself to "toggling," improvisitory attempts to patch up the
unravelling family structure. He is the first to recognize Tag in the
disguise of the Sunlight Man, but he offers Clumly no assistance. Instead he sets off on his own fruitless, and frequently comic, search
across an Indian reservation in the company of a flower-child hitch-
hiker. His son Will Jr. has become the prisoner of a personal obsession,
the pursuit of an elusive swindler, and he never intervenes effectively

in the crisis that claims the lives of his brother and his uncle.

There are several other characters who, although not directly involved in the pursuit of the Sunlight Man, are significant moral presences in the novel. Ben Hodge, the congressman's fourth child, comes closest to being his father's moral heir. Ben is a farmer and a lay preacher who lives in close contact with nature and his fellow man. He has faith in basic human decency, and he acts out this faith by continuing his father's practice of taking wayward youth as foster children. This faith is poorly repaid by the Slater brothers, who turn out to be thieves and murderers, but it does bear fruit in Luke, who recognizes in Ben his true moral father. Sadly, even Ben's deep moral vision is shaken by Tag's death: "His brother was dead, and he could make of it neither an abstract truth nor a story. . . . The final truth, he seemed to understand by this queer twist his brain had taken, had nothing to do with human thought or human story; unspeakable" (665).

Esther Clumly, Fred's blind wife, is another morally sensitive individual at the periphery of the novel's main action. In the darkness of her own soul, she endures her private struggle of anarchy versus order. She must resist the temptations of alcoholism and suicide, as she struggles past religious and sexual doubts. She achieves a kind of order—perhaps only temporary—at the novel's end, but we have seen through her sightless eyes the price she has had to pay. Her struggle bears fruit beyond her personal situation, for Clumly acknowledges in his talk that his wife has been an important moral model for him.

An Uncertain Outcome

What picture emerges from the reflection of the novel's central concerns in the lives of these other characters? How stands the struggle between order and anarchy in this community? The issue is far from certain. We see instances of earnestness, goodness, and sacrifice, but we also see anger, impotence, and isolation. At the novel's end, the best of this lot are either dead (Luke), disillusioned (Ben), or marginally effective (Esther).

The final word in this novel is, once again, the first. As in *The Resurrection,* Gardner begins his novel with a scene that occurs many years after the novel's last incident. The setting is the home of Judge Sam White, the man who succeeded Congressman Hodge as the area's political patriarch. The judge, now retired, receives Fred Clumly, also retired and a widower. The judge holds forth as he has many times before, solemn and oracular, from behind a cloud of tobacco smoke. The judge speaks of entropy and tells us that the final victory has fallen to the forces of anarchy: "nothing in this world is universal any more; there is neither wisdom nor stability, and faithfulness is dead" (5). Clumly does not try to answer, for he has been in the presence of this monologist before and knows that no answer is expected. We get a partial answer from outside the judge's window, where we see spring stirring in the New York air. Old lives are ending and new ones are beginning, but a troubled question remains: has anything been gained?

Clumly's solar metaphor assumes that the setting sun warms and enlightens the community, leaving something of value behind. But if the judge represents the community, it is hard to find the fruit of the tragedy we have witnessed. The judge vaguely remembers a "magician," but he can recall neither Tag's name nor his fate. The sound we hear emerging from this cloud of smoke is the voice of the pompous, indifferent official order against which Tag rebelled. These tired, impersonal mutterings are indeed the voice of entropy. This novel then leaves us with two "last words": Clumly's talk at the novel's end and the judge's verdict rendered years later at the novel's beginning. Most of us, I think, will choose to give priority to Clumly's voice. But we must also, if we wish to honor this novel's complex dialogue, hear these other, much darker and more threatening rumblings.

Chapter Six
Jason and Medeia

Gardner's epic poem, *Jason and Medeia* (1973) is both one of his most ambitious and one of his least understood works. In it he attempts a reworking of the ancient stories of Jason, chief of the Argonauts, and Medeia, the bride he carried back from his famous voyage. Despite Gardner's claim that the poem was one of his three best works,[1] it has, for the most part, been overlooked in discussions of his work. This has been so presumably because it is a poem and not a novel. And yet it is a narrative, and a longer one than all but one of his novels. It is, moreover, an ambitious work that treats many of the familiar Gardnerian themes, such as morality and art.

One of the reasons for the poem's neglect is, I believe, the mediocrity of its verse. Gardner, perhaps aware of this, at moments abandons poetry and reverts to prose. But if his poetic powers fail him, his narrative and dialectical skills do not. Here, as in the novels, we find a narrative that raises, discusses, and tests important issues. Here, as in *Grendel,* we have a modern reworking of a famous epic. But this work is also quite different, for in place of the impious and ironic debunking of the Anglo-Saxon epic, Gardner presents a remarkably straight version of the Greek tragedy. The point of view is not that of the nose-thumbing outsider but of a narrator who is sympathetic with the protagonists.

Dialogue on Several Levels

And yet, despite this, *Jason and Medeia* and *Grendel* are alike in that both open up the monological epic worldview. Gardner does this in his second retelling, first, by juxtaposing two very different sources. The stories of Jason and Medeia occur in numerous classical texts, but Gardner draws primarily from Apollonious of Rhodes's *Voyage of the Argonauts* and from Euripides' *Medeia* and, in fact, makes generous use of translations or near paraphrases of these sources in his own poem. Apollonious' work is an Alexandrian epic whose protagonist, Jason, is a European male, while Euripides' play is a classic tragedy with

Medeia, an Asiatic woman, as its focus. Gardner's poem then has at its
center two conflicting visions and two conflicting sets of values: epic
celebration versus dark tragic despair and the clearheaded practical reason of the Greek leader versus the demonic anger of the barbarian sor-
ceress. Elements previously consigned to separate narratives are here
brought together. Gardner effects this juxtaposition to try to understand how Jason, leader of one of antiquity's most successful epic
quests, could also be the victim of one of its most sanguinary tragedies.
Gardner further opens the story by providing his central characters and
numerous others with vigorous and contentious inner lives. Their conflicting values create a dialogue within the narrative, but Gardner also,
as in *Grendel,* includes a metafictional level that explores the relevance
of this myth to contemporary culture.

Gardner organizes these dialogues on three distinct narrative levels.
The first of these, considered in their historical chronology, draws from
Apollonious. It is the story of Jason's voyage to Kolchis in quest of the
golden fleece and his return to his native Akhaia. The second sequence,
much of which derives from Euripides, is set in Corinth after Jason
and Medeia's flight from Akhaia. Jason presents himself as a candidate
to marry Kreon's daughter and to succeed him on the Corinthian
throne; unfortunately, Medeia learns of this and executes her revenge
on Jason. Jason, as part of his suit to Kreon, recounts his earlier adventures, while Medeia, in her chambers, remembers her version of
these events. In this way, this second level, which is the narrative present of the poem, serves as a frame for the earlier story. In addition to
these two levels, a modern narrator has been transported back to witness the final stages of the tragedy. His actions and comments consti-
tute a third level of narrative and commentary, which is chronologically
simultaneous with the second level. The metafictional reflections on
the myth's contemporary significance derive principally from this third
narrative component.

Jason as Epic Hero

Although Gardner draws primarily from Apollonious for Jason's account of the *Argo's* voyage, he also departs from his source in several
important ways. The first of these is in his presentation of his hero.
Gardner reduces the attention given to Jason's physical exploits and,
at the same time, expands Jason's reflections on them. In so doing, he
solves one of the problems traditionally associated with Apollonious'

Jason, whom readers have often found passionless and hesitant, particularly in contrast with his Homeric forebears. Gardner offers inner views of his protagonist, permitting us to share his thoughts during the voyage and after. Beneath the seemingly passive exterior, we discover a strikingly modern mind: probing, analytical, and skeptical. Gardner expands many of the other Argonauts in the same manner, making them spokesmen for a variety of philosophical attitudes. These points of view further stimulate Jason's reflections and contrast with them in the poem's dialogue. Herakles and Akastos, for instance, defend traditional heroic values such as pity, honor, and love. Several of their fellow adventurers, however, view the world more darkly. The valiant but sardonic Idas sees Zeus, the father of the gods, as brutal and indifferent—"a man-eating spider."[2] Argus, who crafted the famous boat and who joined its crew, has reflected on his experience. For this artisan, the wandering rocks—treacherous volcanic islands that surge unexpectedly from the sea—are a metaphor for our entire universe: dynamic, chaotic, and murderous.

Jason, for the most part, is clearheaded and pragmatic. He is aware of and concerned by the philosophical issues raised by his colleagues, but he avoids the extremes of both grandiloquent idealism and nihilistic despair. His reasons for seeking the golden fleece are never explained by Apollonius, but Gardner, drawing on other classical sources, supplies these motives and, in so doing, establishes at the outset Jason's moderate, practical approach. Jason has seen his uncle usurp the throne of Akhaia, which ought to have passed to him. The teenage Jason, knowing his uncle may try to kill him, realizes he must act. His supporters urge murder and open revolt, but Jason holds back from a solution that would convulse his city in bloody warfare. Peleas, hoping his rival will die in the attempt, offers Jason half of his kingdom if he can capture the golden fleece. The young hero knows the dangers, but he is willing to accept them to recover his birthright without pushing his homeland into civil war.

Jason's many trials will deepen him, provoking him to reflect religiously and philosophically, but they will basically confirm him in his rational and pragmatic approach. When a sequence of miracles following a sacrifice to Hera stirs others to pious enthusiasm, Jason holds back; he seems to sense that the gods can be fickle and that they finally may themselves be subject to other powers. This intuition is strengthened by Phineus, the greatest seer of his time, whom the Argonauts rescue from the Harpies. Phineus offers a somber vision of "dark, unfeeling, unloving powers" (140) controlling human affairs. After listening to Phineus, Jason has a vision of Death who offers this advice: "Fool, you are caught in irrelevant forms: existence as comedy, tragedy, epic. . . . Trust not to seers who conceive no higher force than Zeus. . . . Beware the interstices. There lies thy wreck" (142–43). Jason turns to Mopsos, his augurer, for help in understanding what he has heard. But Mopsos can only sigh, "Who knows? Who cares?" The old man is weary of attempts to understand what is finally unknowable. "Truth," he counsels, "is whatever proves necessary" (143). These auguries and counsels, then, reinforce the pragmatism that becomes the guiding theme of Jason's actions. Jason's goals are to capture the fleece and to return safely to reclaim his throne. He willingly accepts the moral compromises required for these purposes. On Lemnos, for instance, he refuses to avenge men murdered by their wives, and he falsely pledges his love to the leader of these women so that he and his men may have safe passage.

Jason's morality is a major topic of consideration in the second narrative sequence when Jason and the other suitors present their cases to marry Kreon's daughter and to succeed him to the throne. These scenes, it should be pointed out, are one of Gardner's most important additions to the traditional material. They serve, first of all, as the crucial juncture between the stories of Jason the epic hero and Jason the tragic victim. Jason is poised at a critical moment: his epic adventures, which he here recounts, are now behind him; his tragic downfall is in preparation even as he speaks. These scenes of Jason and his competitors provide an opportunity for an open debate on several important issues. Jason's account of his exploits is a deliberate part of his strategy to prove himself the superior candidate. It is also, however, an attempt to be as honest as possible about who and what he is: thus he purposely reveals his religious doubts and moral compromises as well as his heroic achievements.

Jason's case before Kreon is contested by two other suitors, Paidoboron and Koprophoros. Paidoboron, a dark-bearded Scandinavian, sternly condemns Jason's pragmatism and argues for pious submission to the gods. So fervent is his moralism that he soon abandons his own suit and gives over to a general denunciation of cities and civilization. Koprophoros, a corpulent Asian, defends cities but denounces Jason as an artist and as a man. Jason speaks skillfully, Koprophoros concedes, but he is an immoral artist. His narrative undercuts the traditional heroic values and inculcates a corrosive skepticism. He prefers the true artist "who rules words in the fear of God" (176). The questions of art and morality have been important in discussions of Gardner, so we need to look closely at the charges brought by Korprophoros against Jason and at the model, Orpheus, whom he offers as an alternative.

Orpheus is a traditional artist who provides religious reassurance in times of doubt and heroic stimulus in times of battle: when the men are disturbed, he sings of the gods to calm them, and, after Polydeuxes' victory over Amkyos, he composes verses to praise the pugilist's skill. There is, however, one moment when Orpheus' art fails him. As the Argonauts pass the sirens they hear songs totally unlike any they have heard before—songs of "pain and death . . . terrible rages of sex beyond the orgasm, blindness, drunkenness bursting the walls of unconsciousness" (242). Orpheus tries but cannot succeed in blotting the sirens' songs from his comrades' minds, and one of them is pulled over to his death. There are, it seems, dark visions against which Orpheus' traditional moral songs offer scant protection. Orpheus clearly disapproves of his leader, and he withdraws his assistance when he feels to do so might embarrass Jason. Jason knows this, and he attacks Orpheus' facile assumption of moral superiority: "It's easy for the poets to carp at the men who lead. . . . They see all the world as forms to be juxtaposed, proved beautiful. . . . My job's more dull . . . my job is to carry us through" (150).

Koprophoros also charges that Jason is not impartial and that he uses his narrative to advance his own suit. Jason would hardly disagree, since he has been quite frank about his purposes for appearing before Kreon. Koprophoros and Paidoboron, however, have been a good deal less candid. It turns out, they are not even humans at all, but disguised gods, and thus they are far from disinterested themselves in this debate on religious piety. Their reasons for favoring an art that praises the gods are quite understandable, although not entirely "moral," if perfect candor and disinterest are to be the tests of such morality.

Koprophoros challenges not only the morality of Jason's art but of his approach to life, which the god finds too rational and analytical. The moral sense, Koprophoros argues, is grounded at a prerational level of consciousness, and he cites as an instance of this prerational moral sense the instinctive revulsion that all people feel toward cannibalism. Jason is, to be sure, scrupulously logical, perhaps excessively so. Nonetheless, his experience has taught him the dangers of the other extreme. He is, after all, married to Medeia, the embodiment of instinct and passion. The single greatest mistake thus far in his career occurred when he was not sufficiently analytical and subconsciously yielded to his wife's wild designs. After his return to Akhaia, Jason shared power with Peleas, but he was continually frustrated by him when he attempted progressive reforms. Medeia—who clearly does not share Koprophoros's instinctive aversion to cannibalism—contrived to aid her husband by killing Peleas and serving his flesh at dinner. Jason, who was ignorant of his wife's plans, realizes later that she correctly sensed and acted on his unconscious desires. These experiences only strengthen Jason's suspicion of feelings as a moral guide.

Kreon listens intently to Jason's presentation and recognizes a fellow spirit. He also has witnessed tragedy and knows the calculations and compromises required of those who wield power. He accepts Jason as his heir. A gifted successor to the Corinthian crown is assured, and Jason's search for a throne is at an end. And yet it all goes up in the smoke of Medeia's incendiary wrath. What went wrong? Where is the flaw in Jason and Kreon's eminently reasonable pragmatism?

Jason as Tragic Victim

A partial answer is incorporated into the structure of this second narrative sequence. As Jason puts his case, recounting his famous adventures, Medeia, alone in her chambers, relives the same experiences and recounts her version of them. She is a witch who has been granted knowledge of the gods' actions, and thus she can begin her account with the divine rivalries that led Hera, Athena, and Aphrodite to assist Jason's quest. The goddesses cause Medeia to fall in love with the Argonaut leader so that she will betray her family and assist him. She is for them a thing, a tool in their machinations, and her description of herself in the third person during this portion of her narrative suggests their casual indifference to her. Her sudden shift to the first person at the moment she first sees Jason renders the power of that moment and reminds us that it is a thinking and feeling human being who is being manipulated in this scene. After this moment her fate is sealed. She will be driven by her divinely inspired passion to increasingly barbaric acts: the betrayal of her father, the murder of her brother, the killing of Peleas, and finally her terrible revenge against Jason, Kreon, Pyripta, and even her own children. Her narrative alternates with Jason's coolly rational account, and it provides an ominous and ironic counterpoint to it. Her story suggests that there are dark convulsive powers beyond all human calculation that can erupt to destroy the lives of guilty and innocent alike.

Jason reveals his fatal flaw when he fails to prevent Kreon's execution of Amekhenos, the son of a man who aided the Argonauts. Jason, coldly reviewing his options, decides that the lesser good he can do for this individual is outweighed by the greater good he will be able to accomplish after he wins Kreon's favor. A god, seeing this and speaking through a mortal, correctly judges Jason's deficiency as "shallowness of heart" (274). The problem with Jason's seemingly reasonable calculation is not just its insensitivity to Amekhenos's suffering. Being reasonable, Jason cannot anticipate the disproportionate outrage this act will inspire among the Corinthians, triggering a bloody revolt against both Jason and Kreon. Even more disastrous, Jason's logical survey cannot begin to fathom the depths of Medeia's demonic anger; he seems genuinely to believe that she will agree that his remarriage and accession to the throne is in her best interest and in the best interest of their sons. Jason's view is shallow in that it assumes reality's surface is solid and that we can rationally plot our course across it. But that apparently solid surface contains dangerous gaps—the interstices of which he was warned—and these gaps can open and swallow us. Jason's reasonableness carries with it a curious lack of passion; this emotional shallowness plays him false when Medeia murders Pyripta. Medeia decides that if Jason plunges in heedlessly to rescue his bride and dies with her, she will spare his sons. He hangs back, and she adds his children to the list of her victims.

But this is not the end, for Gardner carries on beyond where Apollonious and Euripides leave off. We watch Jason, in Idas and Lynkeus's company, resolutely pursue Medeia. On a deserted island the travelers come upon Oidipus who shares with them the wisdom he has gathered. He has known most of the great heroes, and the lessons of their lives are inconclusive. The faithless Theseus and the pious Herakles, the virtuous Aeneas and the rancorous Akhilles—all knew tragedy in their careers. Only Odysseus—for Oidipus, the least deserving of all—lived a reasonably painfree life. Their lessons provide little help for one seeking a clear and consistent morality. "The lives of men," Oidipus concludes, "confute each other, nothing is stable, nothing" (350). Oidipus, for his part, wishes only to forget this life and to drift, willless, toward death.

Oidipus seeks to question Jason, for he guesses that Jason may be a harbinger of large changes occurring in the world. Jason has had a

similar intuition about himself on the eve of Medeia's revenge. He
realized that he is different from other heroes and that he is part of a
transformation taking place. He has rejected blind religious piety and,
facing the world honestly, has affirmed *human* values: "I've walked,
cold-bloodedly honest, to the rim of the pit. I've affirmed justice, compassion, decency. When granted power I've used it to benefit man. I've
fiercely denied that life is bestial—having seen in my own life the leer
of the ape." He knows these views place him in danger, but he pledges
to remain faithful to his rebellious vision: "The sky turns dark, and
gods threaten me. If the universe is evil, then let me be martyred in
battle with the universe" (277). Jason, as Gardner conceives him, is a
strikingly contemporary figure. He stands as a forerunner of modern
humanism: secular, rational, and pragmatic. As the poem nears its
close we are led to consider what might be the consequences of the
cultural transformation that Jason anticipates. The poem suggests a
partial answer, since its third level of narration is set more than three
thousand years after the epoch portrayed in the two other levels.

The poem's narrator is a bookish modern man—perhaps a classics
professor—who witnesses the entire poem in a long night's vision. It
can hardly be said that the world he knows is superior to Jason's, for
the narrator sees the suffering of Jason's sons repeated in modern ref-
ugee camps and watches the flames of Thebes merge with the glow of
modern cities under siege. He identifies intensely with both Jason and
Medeia and tries to warn them, but to no avail. Near the poem's end,
he is lifted beyond the human world to view the world of the gods.
He is at first entranced by the graceful dance of figures representing
Vision, Love, and Life. He is appalled, however, when these figures
turn out to be Athena, Aphrodite, and Hera, the goddesses whose
schemings have controlled Jason and Medeia's destinies. He watches in
horror as these three prepare the tragedy's sanguinary conclusion. He
turns to Artemis, who had been his sympathetic guide, only to recoil
when he sees her metamorphose into the witch Hekate. The narrator
tries desperately to intervene with the gods, lecturing them on the
enlightened teachings of the Hindus and Schopenhauer, Chaucer and
Shakespeare, Chia Yi and Dante, but to no effect. He is obviously
frightened that a whole tradition of Eastern and Western humanism
may be powerless against divine indifference. This fear becomes even
more apparent when he meets his own double, and this double articulates his deepest concerns to him: "I see traces of a fear that literature
may be nothing but a game, and stark reality the chaos remaining

when the last game's played." The narrator, in anguish, asks, "Is nothing serious?" (313); the only response he receives is his own voice's forlorn echo.

Epic and Tragic Voices in Dialogue

The narrator's visit to Olympus brings to a focus the issues raised for Gardner by Jason and Medeia's stories. Which of the visions left us by our Greek ancestors is finally most profound: the epic's affirmation of heroic action or tragedy's chastened resignation to inevitable decay? Gardner clearly felt a strong fascination with the epic world, evidenced by his turning to it in this poem, in *Grendel* and in the translation of *Gilgamesh* on which he collaborated. He had the honesty in *Grendel* to challenge the epic perspective with the views of the outsider, which the epic's nationalistic celebration necessarily excludes. Here he challenges it from within our tradition by setting against it the competing vision of the tragic poet. The narrator, who struggles in this scene to resist the full implications of that despairing vision, dramatizes the poem's central questions. Is the ultimate reality meaningless chaos, and, if so, is all human activity simply vain and empty posturing?

The scene also, I believe, dramatizes the poem's answer or, rather, answers. For here we are poised between several possibilities. We can imagine the narrator, despite all that he has seen, clinging tenaciously to his humanistic faith. We must also, however, imagine his double laughing sarcastically at this tenacity. This strategy of positioning us between opposite possibilities occurs again in the poem's final lines. We and the narrator are on the desert island with Jason, Idas, and Oidipus. Jason receives the blind king's blessing and, driven on by love, sets out to retrieve Medeia. As the voyagers set sail the sky is filled with exploding lights that may signify "some great celebration" or, alternatively, "some final, maniacal war" (353). Out of the darkness, the narrator hears Jason break his silence, "Nothing is impossible! Nothing is definite!" Jason then reaffirms his heroic code, "Be calm! Be brave!" We then hear Oidipus repeat the first two phrases ("Nothing is impossible, nothing is definite!"), but the conclusion that he draws—"Be still!" (353)—is tragic resignation. The narrator tells us that he witnessed these events in a world of old graves where "King Dionysos-Christ refused to die," but where "deep in the night old snakes were coupling with murderous intent" (354). It is for us to choose who will be triumphant.

Chapter Seven
Nickel Mountain

Nickel Mountain (1973) differs from Gardner's other novels in a number of ways. First, there is the importance accorded to the novel's setting. Gardner, of course, quite skillfully used the country surrounding Batavia, New York, as the setting for *The Resurrection* and *The Sunlight Dialogues,* and he even used elements of it symbolically, as in the lofty hilltop setting for Congressman Hodge's estate. But Nickel Mountain, the promontory to which the novel's title refers, is more than a background for its action and more than an incidental symbol: it provides a brooding moral atmosphere for the novel and, at moments, almost becomes a character in it, provoking the other characters to reflection and influencing their behavior.

The Mountain and Its People

This mountain and its neighbors in New York's Catskills have many moods. There are dark woods, threatening swamps, and treacherous fogs; snows linger well into spring and are replaced by oppressive summer heat and drought. But, seen at the proper moment, in the proper light, the landscape can seem generous and welcoming. The fertile valleys, carefully maintained by its farmers, are an American Eden, the perfect integration of man and a beneficent nature that the book's subtitle—"A Pastoral Novel"—leads us to expect. The mountain's contrasting moods—threatening and provident—provide an apt synecdoche for the complex lives lived in its shadow.

When we turn to these lives and to the characters who live them, we discover a second difference between this novel and Gardner's other fiction. The characters here are much less given to overt intellectual disputation; there are no James Chandlers, no Agathons, and no Sunlight Men among the simple farmers, housewives, and professional people who live near the mountain. Despite the lack of conscious philosophical discussion, this novel is no less dialogical than its predecessors. Each of the characters embodies a distinct set of attitudes and values, which are brought into contact with the values of other characters. The novel's episodic structure—it is really eight individually

62

titled vignettes—assists this purpose. It enables us to get extended views, inner as well as outer, of seemingly minor characters, thus extending and amplifying the moral options represented within the novel. The recurring characters, the developing drama of the main characters, and the reappearance of important themes draw the individual vignettes into a novelistic whole.

Let us now look more closely at these characters and the themes posed by their lives. The most important of these characters are Henry Soames, the middle-aged proprietor of a diner, and Callie Wells, a teenager who comes to work for him. Henry marries Callie when she becomes pregnant and is abandoned by her lover, Willard Freund; together Henry and Callie raise her son, Jimmie, and come to love one another. Other characters include Callie's parents: Frank Wells, an agnostic who prays during a moment of emergency, and Eleanor Wells, a Christian who refuses to love her neighbor. There are also George Loomis, a crippled farmer, and Doc Cathey, the local doctor: both are misanthropists who, nonetheless, seek out the company of the regulars at Henry's diner. Finally, there are Simon Bale, a fanatical fundamentalist lay preacher and the Goat Lady, a mentally deficient itinerant; both die and become precipitants in the novel's crises.

The central situation resembles that of *The Resurrection*. Henry Soames suffers from heart disease and, like James Chandler, knows that he will soon die. He is, however, more successful than Chandler in using his final days to change his life significantly: he bestirs himself from his moral torpor, joins his life with Callie's, and awakens to a richer, more responsible—and sometimes more painful—existence. Henry and Callie's stories and the contrasting stories of their neighbors enable Gardner to explore a number of related questions. How do we understand and communicate with other humans? How do we live full and responsible lives? What, finally, is the meaning of our experience? Is it absurd, or is it holy? Gardner constructs a dialogue on these questions, filtering them through individual lives and consciousnesses. The various characters represent different responses to the questions posed, and while some responses are preferable to others, none represents an absolute ideal. Here, as elsewhere in Gardner's novels, even the less attractive characters are treated with sensitivity and compassion.

Understanding and Communication

The problem of human understanding is posed with particular acuity for the people who gather at the Stop-Off Diner by the sudden appearance of Simon Bale. Bale is rendered homeless by a fire that also kills his wife, but his Bible-pounding fanaticism alienates most of the community, and he receives scant sympathy. The single exception is Henry Soames, who takes Bale in and even pays the cost of his wife's funeral. Henry does not have the luxury of his friends' instinctive responses, for he has the crucial Gardnerian virtue of imaginative identification. He manages to project himself into the most unsympathetic consciousnesses and to see, at least momentarily, from that perspective: "his premise, deeper than judgment, something in his blood by now, was that somehow even the most outrageous behavior . . . must make some kind of reasonable, human sense. He'd work that sense out, eventually, finding good even in the most unthinkable points of view."[1] Thus he senses the inner life and pain not only of Bale, but of George Loomis and Doc Cathey as well. Although Callie initially shares her mother's distrust, under Henry's example she grows more tolerant and also accepts Simon. Unfortunately, the narrative shows that Henry's compassion is hardly an unmixed blessing. Bale never acknowledges Henry's generosity and, in fact, abuses it by frightening Jimmy with threats of the devil. Simon's death eventually burdens Henry and Callie with a guilt that provokes one of the novel's crises.

Closely related to the problem of understanding is the problem of communication. Many of the members of this community who gather at the diner seem as frozen in their abilities to communicate as they are in their compassion. They are content to trade clichés or commonplace observations about the weather, farming, or politics. Such exchanges offer them the comfort of the familiar and protection against embarrassingly direct self-disclosure. Simon Bale represents the negative extreme of this communication by set phrase: he speaks almost exclusively in biblical quotations. Doc Cathey wittily confounds him with conflicting quotations, but he also has his stock of verbal tics. George Loomis, for his part, meets every situation with a cynical wisecrack, such as the blasphemous "Jesus please us" (51). Willard Freund, upon his return from the university, proves that he has mastered the vocabulary of academic cant.

Language, for these people, seems more a hindrance than a help in communication. Henry particularly labors against this obstacle; his thoughts and feelings often seem to exceed his ability to put them into words, and thus we frequently find him in moments of frustrated, inarticulate hand waving. The amazing and reassuring thing is that, despite these obstacles, communication does happen. Early in the novel

Henry and an old man named Kuzitski engage in a slightly comic exchange of drunken clichés; it is clear, however, that, despite its clumsiness, each of the speakers senses the other's deep loneliness. Henry and Callie provide the most significant instances of this intuitive communication. Henry's proposal of marriage to Callie is never expressed directly in the book nor is her acceptance; words seem unnecessary: her need is clear to him, his generosity is evident to her, and so they act. Not only do they understand what is not said, they also understand when what is said is the opposite of what is really felt. Near the end of her long and agonizing labor, Callie cries out that she hates Henry and loves another. Henry is not disturbed; he waits patiently until after the childbirth when Callie, indirectly, sends word of her love and respect. What makes such wordless communication possible is the sympathetic understanding we have discussed earlier. In the course of their time together, Henry and Callie grow in their abilities to imaginatively identify and thus to understand instinctively, without words.

Experiences in Time

This capacity for growth is the central fact in Henry and Callie's lives and the point that most distinguishes them from their friends. The qualitative difference this brings in Henry and Callie's lives can be seen most clearly in the temporal experiences their lives embrace. In many ways the tiny farm community seems to stand outside of time: each year is "like last year and the year before—and a hundred thousand years before that" (25). But this seeming timelessness is not idyllic but tragic, for the residents can not escape physical decay, only moral growth. Doc Cathey freezes himself in the stylized gestures of the avuncular country doctor, "an old man pretending the years brought wisdom they hadn't brought" (168). George Loomis, on the other hand, is always the wisecracking cynic; time brings physical deterioration—he loses a leg, then an arm—but no true development. Willard Freund's problem is not suspended animation but regression: when life at the university proves unsettling he returns to his parents and "the land of his innocence" (273). Simon Bale has withdrawn into his own version of eternal religious time, interpreting all secular experiences in terms of divine final judgment.

Henry and Callie, before their marriage, inhabit the world of dull routine where each day and each experience is qualitatively indistinguishable from those that preceded it. In the novel's second paragraph Gardner describes Henry in a scene that captures his existence during this stage of his life:

Sometimes when he was not in a mood to read he would stand at the window and watch the snow. On windy nights the snow hurtled down through the mountain's darkness and into the blue-white glow of the diner and the pink glitter of the neon sign and away again into the farther darkness and the woods on the other side of the highway. Henry Soames would pull at his lip with his thumb and his first finger, vaguely afraid of the storm and vaguely drawn by it. . . . Though he stood in the lean-to-room behind the diner he could hear the hum of the diner clock, and sometimes he would see in his mind the red and blue hands and, unaware of what he was doing, would try to make out what time it was—twelve, one, quarter-to-three. (3)

Gardner here uses what Gérard Genette calls the *iterative*.[2] This mode presents many similar events as a single occurrence. The signs of the iterative in this passage are the temporal modifiers *sometimes* and *on windy nights,* and the use of the conditional instead of the past tense. These elements indicate that the event, which in other respects is described as a unique event, has actually happened many times. Unlike summary, which abstracts and presents the general features of many events, the iterative presents the event concretely and specifically, while noting its repetitive quality. The result, as Genette has shown in his analysis of Proust, is both a narrative freshness and a timeless quality of an individual caught in a pattern of endless repetition. Henry's dreamy winter reverie, his confusion about the hour, and the fact that this event is part of a pattern of similar events suggest the immobility of Henry's life before Callie enters it. It is a life of routine, each day like the preceding, without any moments of transcendence or real intensity.

All this changes when Henry joins his life to Callie's. The novel's second and third chapters dramatize the qualitative difference this change brings. These chapters deal with Henry and Callie's marriage and with the birth of their child. The novel's eight chapters cover roughly five and a half years; its first chapter covers seven months, and most of the other chapters cover fairly generous periods. The second and third chapters—as well as the final chapter, which we will discuss later—cover single events. In chapter 2 the time covered is less than a day, and in chapter 3 it is forty-eight hours. The isolation of each of these events in a separate chapter and the amount of narrative attention given them indicate their importance in Henry and Callie's emotional and moral lives. These events contrast with all other events in their lives in terms of the temporal experiences they embody.

Chapter 2 presents the wedding and a transcendent, sacramental experience in time. We view the wedding and its preparations through Callie's mind. As she waits in her parents' living room for the car that will take her to church, she remembers the other weddings she has seen. As she does so, she realizes the uniqueness of the event about to happen and its transforming spiritual significance: "Again and again she had watched them come down the aisle, transfigured, radiating beauty like Christ on the mountain, lifted out of mere humanness into their perfect eternal instant. . . . They went up the aisle white forms, insubstantial as air, poised in the instant of total freedom like the freedom of angels, between child and adult, between daughter and wife, and they came down transformed to reality, married: in one split second, in a way, grown-up" (71).

Although this passage describes many occurrences, it is not the dull repetition of the same action in one life; it is a unique event, occurring once in a lifetime, to many different individuals. It is a ritual experience lifting the individual out of an isolated instant into a tradition, a cultural experience shared by many over the years. For a Christian like Callie, it is also a sacramental moment transporting the individual into an eternal moment in the life of Christ and his church. This is not, however, Simon Bale's notion of the sacred as something divorced from the world and existing only in the mind of God; rather it is the sacred embodied here and now in the holy, physical union of man and woman. Despite last minute doubts, Callie goes on with the marriage. As she walks into the candle-lit, flower-perfumed church the special, transcendent moment occurs for her: "she walked slowly, having all eternity to taste the strange new sensation of freedom, knowing that she too was beautiful now, yes, more beautiful than the wedding gown, lighter, purer, immutable" (83).

Such sacramental experiences are, necessarily, rare and brief. As the wedding ends, Callie already feels herself being drawn into another experience of time. The pull she feels is the life she and Henry are about to begin, and, although it will be filled with routine, it cannot be like the lives they led before. They have been changed by the com-

mitments they made to one another and to the child stirring within
Callie. These commitments give greater significance to daily activities
and heightened intensity to certain shared experiences.

We have an example of this intensity in chapter 3. Chapter 2 and
the wedding briefly lift the couple out of time into an eternal transcendent moment. Chapter 3 goes in the opposite direction, plunging
them into the painful duration of intensively lived time. Callie's labor
drags on for many torturous hours, eventually requiring a cesarean delivery. References to time are infrequent in the novel and nonexistent
in the preceding wedding chapter. Here they are frequent—at least
fifteen references to the slowly passing minutes during Callie's hours
of misery. We experience these hours from Henry's point of view, and
thus we follow in vivid detail his fevered drive to the hospital over
snow-packed roads, his sleepless night in the waiting room, and his
reactions to Callie's screams and recriminations.

This immersion in the physical experience of time lived under great
pain and pressure is the opposite of the wedding's temporal transcendence. Taken together, they represent the qualitative extremes of the
life the couple has begun together and a contrast with the numbness
they have left behind. No other characters in the novel are described
experiencing these extremes, and it is difficult to imagine them doing
so. The juxtaposition of these two experiences in these two consecutive
chapters suggests that the experiences go together, that one is the price
of the other: the transcendent must be paid for by an intense living of
life in the moment. The sharing of such an experience of lived time
marks one as permanently as the sacramental experience described earlier. Henry glimpses this fact after the child's birth. He worries about
Willard Freund, the baby's biological father, as he considers a set of
dominoes left in the hospital waiting room. Our experiences in time,
he decides, are like a row of dominoes that, in failing, touch one another, passing the initial impulse down the line. A domino outside the
row does not feel that impulse and does not participate in the moment
it creates. Willard has withdrawn and has not been part of the events
surrounding his son's birth. Henry has participated and, biology aside,
is more intimately bound to Callie and Jimmy than is Willard.

Responsibility, Commitment, and Faith

Henry and Callie's willingness to commit themselves—to accept responsibility for their acts and for others—lifts their lives above those

around them. This theme is important, for it is around such commitments, or their refusal, that the novel's crises turn. The main line of action is initiated by Willard Freund's refusal to accept responsibility for Callie's pregnancy. Simon Bale offers his own variation on this theme of refused responsibility when he piously disdains to arrange his wife's burial, leaving matters in God's—and Henry's—hands. Doc Cathey is more responsible, acting both as the community's doctor and its justice of the peace. But he carefully restricts his engagement to the formal boundaries of these two roles. He washes his hands of Simon.

George Loomis represents a potentially tragic variant on this theme. He has withdrawn, wounded in body and spirit, to his isolated farm on Crow Mountain. He has his friends at the diner, but he carefully calibrates the responsibility he will accept for them. When Henry offers his life savings to George if he will marry Callie, George promptly says no. George faces a deeper crisis when he accidentally kills the Goat Lady. He refuses to tell anyone, less, we imagine, from fear of prosecution than from a reluctance to open his private life to others. He suffers from his lonely guilt, and the environment seems to respond to the unacknowledged crime with parching heat and drought. George cannot consciously resolve his private suffering, but his unconscious does it for him. As the farmers wait for rain at the diner, George blurts out a remark about the Goat Lady. He subsequently denies any knowledge of her, but Callie guesses the truth about what has happened. She also guesses that George's unintentional admission has saved him and the others. As if to ratify Callie's intuition, the heavens open up that evening, ending the physical—and perhaps spiritual—drought that has gripped the community.

Henry is the positive variant on the theme of responsibility. He accepts responsibility where others have refused it: for Callie, for Jimmy, for Simon, and for Simon's wife. But this positive example is more complex than it first seems, for Henry pushes responsibility too far, burdening himself with a guilt that is not properly his. He lacerates himself for weeks over Simon's accidental death, imagining ways he could have avoided it. Here George Loomis provides a salutary measure of cold realism. He accuses Henry of wanting to inculpate himself for Simon's accident rather than to admit that it was the result of blind chance that no one could have prevented. Such an admission would make the world seem absurd and human life pointless. Henry subconsciously claims responsibility for Simon's death to rescue his belief in an ordered universe where humans can act responsibly.

This discussion of responsibility has brought us to the fundamental belief that most sets Henry apart—his religious faith. Bale is, of course, fanatically religious, but his is a neurotic conviction that causes him to dismiss the world entirely. Callie's mother is an active church-goer, but her faith does not seem to make her more compassionate or loving. Her husband and Doc Cathey have lapsed into indifferent agnosticism. Callie's faith is deep and active, but it is not particularly reflective. Henry and George stand closest together, for although they fundamentally disagree, they have both thought long and hard about their experiences. Their differences are dramatized in a remembered exchange about Henry's family. The issue, once again, is responsibility. George speaks first:

"You take on a responsibility like that, and you say to yourself you'll move heaven and earth to protect the kid you love, or the woman, or whoever it happens to be, but the minute you say it you're forgetting something."
    "What's that?" Henry had said. George Loomis stared down into the night, leaning forward over the steering wheel, and he said, "You can't."
    "It's what drives you to God," Henry said with a little laugh.
    George too had laughed, like a murderer. (173)

Both men understand that beneath the moral commitment to other lives lies a deeper, often unstated, commitment to an ordered universe, a commitment, in effect, to God. George—maimed in body and spirit—can make neither commitment. Henry, more fortunate, makes both.

The Mountain as Presence

The question of Henry's religious belief brings us back to the mountain, which stands as the symbol of the novel's spiritual as well as its physical environment. Henry, of all the novel's characters, feels most comfortable in the mountain's presence. He lives at its base, it is true, while George lives on the slopes of the neighboring Crow Mountain; but George—who has drawn into the dark forests like a wounded animal—actually fears the mountains. His paranoia causes him, at least once, to approach his own house on his belly, his rifle in hand. Henry, on the other hand, feels a deep kinship with the enveloping hills. He spends long hours walking them, hunting or simply musing in their deep fogs. He can see Nickel Mountain from his living room window, and he can consider its moods and their implications for his own life:

(the trees and hills were like something alive, not threatening, exactly, because Henry had known them all his life, but not friendly, either: hostile, but
not in any hurry, conscious that time was on their side: they would bury him,
for all his size and for all his undeniable harmlessness, and even his own
troublesome, alien kind would soon forget him, and the mountains would
bury them too.) In his present mood, watching sunset come on, he felt at one
with the blue-treed mountains, and at one, equally, with the man in the
dimness behind him. (153)

Looking out on Nickel Mountain's dark slopes, Henry understands
and embraces the fundamental order they seem to figure. He admires
the mountain's somber majesty, but he knows that, finally, it is indifferent to his own doomed mortality. He accepts this fact and, in so
doing, feels a kinship with everything bathed by the setting sun. He
also draws from it the serenity and confidence to act responsibly. The
man whom he glimpses in the dim light and with whom he feels bound
in a common mortality is Simon Bale. These reflections will be followed by Henry's sympathetic identification with Simon and with his
decision to offer him shelter. In this scene the themes of man's relationship to nature and his relationship to his fellow man are united.

Henry's intuition of a divine order is hardly without qualifying
doubts, but it is strengthened by his life with Callie. Reflecting on
their years together, he realizes how they have helped him to see the
world "less as a yarn told after dinner . . . and more as a kind of church
service—communion, say, or a wedding" (299–300). More and more
aware of the "the holiness of things" (302), Henry visits a local church.
Repelled by its smug parishioners and their harsh doctrines, he withdraws quickly. The holiness he discovers is not that of organized religion but one grounded in an acceptance of our mortal condition and
the love that makes it worthwhile.

Waiting for Death

The novel then, out of the many voices in its dialogue, gives particular emphasis to Henry Soames's. But this affirmation is qualified and
put into perspective in the novel's final scene. This scene, which brings
back and modulates many of the novel's themes, is set in a graveyard
on the side of Nickel Mountain. Henry came here as a boy with his

father and still comes to visit his parents' graves and to reflect. Today
he has come hunting rabbits with his son. Henry kills a rabbit and
then discovers that he must explain death to the four-year old. This
morbid theme continues when they come upon an aged couple exhum-
ing their son buried fifty years earlier. They are leaving the area and
wish to take the body with them. Henry and Jimmy watch and listen
as the aged pair continue a long standing quarrel:

"I tell Walt it don't much matter where he lays," the woman said, "his soul's
in Glory." . . .
   The old man waved at her as if to hit her. "Oh, shut up," he said. Then,
to Henry: "She's crazy. Always has been."
   "Walt don't believe in God," the old woman said. She smiled, sly, still
looking at the ground. . . .
   "He's dead and rotten," the old man said. . . . "Now, you shut up."
(306–7)

Once again we hear the themes of understanding, communication,
marriage, and religious faith, but here these themes are inflected neg-
atively. The difference between this couple and Henry and Callie is
that the former have been married fifty years, the latter barely five.
The older couple have suffered a tragic blow early in their life together:
their only child was struck by lightning and killed. This couple, appearing at the novel's end, throws a retrospective shadow over the
younger one. Could Henry and Callie's love stand up over a half a
century? Could it withstand a blow as fatal and as absurd as that lightning bolt? Henry tries to intervene between the quarreling pair: he
begins a remark about love and then breaks off in midsentence, realizing his impotence to offer any consolation for a half century of
bitterness.
   The scene continues. The workmen open the grave, lower a chain,
and slowly winch out the dirt-caked coffin. For a tense moment the
rotting box hangs precariously, threatening to deposit its decomposed
contents at Henry and Jimmy's feet. The exit from the grave is a grisly
parody of the resurrection theme, frequent in Gardner's fiction and seen
here in Henry and Callie's rebirth in love. The workmen manage to
get the coffin on the truck, and Jimmy asks if he can join them in
viewing its contents. His father says no. The boy, who has been allowed to handle the dead rabbit, cannot understand; he becomes angry
and accuses his father of not loving him. Here is how the novel ends:

Henry clenched his jaws; but looking at the boy's face, seeing beyond any possible doubt that however trivial the cause, however ridiculous the words, the child's grief was perfectly real, the injustice terrible and never-to-be-forgotten, he bent down to him and said, "Now listen, Jimmy. I love you and you know it. Now quit that crying."

"Well *I* don't love *you*," Jimmy said, not looking at him, seeing what would happen.

Henry smiled sadly, reaching out to touch Jimmy's shoulder. "Poor dreamer," he said.

He was tired and it was a long way back. He thought how good it would be to lie down, only for a little while, and rest. (313)

The novel ends with a final act of love by Henry. It affirms that act but offers no guarantees about its universal applicability. There are some—the old couple, George Loomis, Simon Bale—who have been so wounded by life as to make such love difficult or impossible. Nor does it guarantee its efficacy; Henry has no assurances about the effects of his gesture in Jimmy's life. One thing does seem certain: Jimmy is a dreamer if he believes that he will be able to escape love and the pains it exacts. Henry, for his part, is weary and welcomes the rest that will soon, permanently, be his.

Chapter Eight
October Light

October Light (1976), Gardner admitted, was planned as a novel commemorating the American bicentennial. It should not surprise us, then, that this novel explores, more directly than any other of his works, the values that are fundamental to American society. James Page, an irascible, intensely conservative Vermont farmer, has driven his more liberal sister into her room. The issues that divide them—the Vietnam War, minority rights, feminism—are the issues that divided American society in the seventies. As their quarrel escalates, other members of their rural New England community are drawn in. The novel shows how this microcosm of small-town America deals with personal and political conflict during one of the most inflamed periods in recent American history. On the occasion of America's two-hundredth birthday, Gardner wrote a novel exploring the values of dialogue, understanding, and reconciliation, which are essential to American democracy.

The Central Conflict

October Light's structure, in keeping with its theme, is dialogical. This dialogue occurs both within the narrative and on a metafictional level. In the first instance, the narrative presents a range of characters representing a variety of opinions and temperaments. These attitudes are tested in the working out of the novel's plot. There are at least a half-dozen characters whose values require our attention. The most important of these is James Page himself. More than a half century of working the rocky Vermont soil has instilled in James the virtues of industry, thrift, and independence. Unfortunately, it has also made him intolerant and xenophobic. He had always been irascibly judgmental, bullying his wife, Ariah, and his son, Richard, but in recent years he has become much worse. He now castigates labor unions, social security, and Catholics, as well as Jews, Mexicans, and women. The climax of his angry intolerance occurs just before the novel begins when he fires his shotgun into his sister's television set and, a little later, drives her into her room with a wooden club. He will continue to menace her in this fashion through much of the novel.

After the rupture, James laments his situation. Sally, who has come to live with him after her husband's death, has, James maintains, dispossessed him of his home. She is like the Mafia or Arab terrorists; he has been reduced to a forgotten hired hand on his own property. The facts are quite different. The house and farm, it is true, are James's legal property. His parents left them to James because Sally was married and, so they thought, provided for. Ginny, James's daughter, points out that her grandparents would not have made such a disposition had they known Sally would have been left a destitute widow; Sally, she implies, has a strong moral claim to live in her parents' house. Actually, both could have had their own houses. James had acquired a second house, through marriage, but he set fire to it after his son's death. In any case, Sally has not asked for the entire house, but only to share it with James in exchange for doing his cooking and cleaning.

Gradually the reader realizes that James's intemperate behavior is rooted in his unresolved feelings about his son's death. James wanted Richard to be as tough and self-reliant as he, but the boy could not meet these standards. Rather than accept the boy on his own terms, James bullies him mercilessly and blames him for his younger brother's accidental death. When Richard, as a young man, contributes to a second accidental death, he slumps into deep despondency. His father, not understanding his son's problem, angrily slaps him, and Richard hangs himself. James tries to push all thoughts of guilt from his consciousness—although they surface in a moment of drunkenness—and he continues to insist that the rugged values he imposed on his son were the only correct ones. To do otherwise would be to admit that he had been mistaken and had bullied his son to suicide. Late in the novel, James faces his guilt and the consequences of his "petty-minded notion of truth."[1]

The Voices of James Page

The reader also realizes that, despite his intemperate behavior, there is much that is admirable in James. First of all, he does more than merely preach self-reliance, he actually practices it, working the unyielding Vermont soil in all weathers. The hard work and solitude have made him reflective, and he reveals in quieter moments a philosophical, even tragic, sense of life. James is then, like many of Gardner's characters, a complex and divided individual. The divisions here are dramatized in two voices, which we can hear in the passages narrated through James's consciousness. The omniscient narrator enters the minds of different characters at different times, and when he enters James's consciousness he often uses James's own language to present his thoughts. Here are James's reflections on why he destroyed his sister's television:

He'd done plenty for his sister, had walked his mile and a half and then some. But he had, like any man, his limit, and the limit was TV. God made the world to be looked at head on, and let a bear live in the woodshed, he'd soon have your bed. It was matter of plain right and wrong, that was all. The Devil finds work for empty heads. "Did God give the world His Holy Word in television pictures?" he'd asked her, leering. "*No* sir," he'd answered himself, "used print!" (4–5)

The last two sentences are the only direct quotes, yet we have the impression that we are hearing James's voice throughout. This is because the diction, syntax, and imagery of the entire passage seem to belong to James and to his distinctive worldview. The sentences, for the most part, are short and declarative, with little subordination; the diction is simple, and the imagery derives from the land and from the Bible: taken together they suggest a clearheaded and uncomplicated approach to the world. This simplicity is the product of years of experience, not only of James, but of generations of rural New Englanders reducing their wisdom to lapidary formulations about man, nature, and God. As a consequence, this passage turns out to be largely a sequence of set phrases—clichés and aphorisms—which are announced as self-evident or divinely revealed truths. They move through James's mind with such ease because they have been thoroughly assimilated and require no reflection. The language here is clearly not the language of dialogue, and we are not surprised to discover James smugly answering his own question to his sister. The narrator frequently uses similar diction, syntax, and imagery to present James's consciousness in the novel's first chapter. Regionalism like "meaner than pussley broth" (4) and "by tunkit" (7) abound in this section. It is significant, however, that when James's grandson asks him what "pussley broth" and "tunkit" mean, he does not know or will not say. James's use of the archaic regional dialect is a linguistic tropism: he is less concerned with communicating to outsiders than with affirming his solidarity with the past and with this isolated region.

Fortunately, James can also think in another idiom. He is, in fact, quite curious about language, and he even keeps a pocket notebook to jot down words that interest him. Here is a portion of his reflections prompted by a consideration of the words *down* and *up*:

> Everything decent, James Page believed, supported the struggle upward, gave strength to the battle against gravity. And all things foul gave support not to gravity—there was nothing inherently evil in stone or a holstein bull—but to the illusion of freedom and ascent. The Devil's visions were all dazzle and no lift, mere counterfeit escape, the lightness of a puffball—flesh without nutrients—the lightness of a fart, a tale without substance, escape from the world of hard troubles and grief in a spaceship. (12)

We are struck, first of all, by the sensitivity of the philosophical reflection. The preceding invective against the modern world would not have prepared us for this. Equally striking is the language: the diction is more literate and the syntax more sophisticated than in the passage dominated by the regional idiom. We note, for instance, the longer sentences, the parallelisms, the inserted elements, and the biblical inversion of "all things foul." We might not recognize it immediately as James's had the narrator not introduced it as part of James's meditation. The earthy, even vulgar images and the religious references should, however, reassure us that it is the same mind that we explored earlier. James, then, is a complex character with different levels of consciousness and, correspondingly, with different linguistic voices. The voices here, however, are fewer and less divergent than those found in *Grendel,* and they do not result in the cacophonous internal dialogue from which that tragic outsider suffers. In James the two voices remain relatively separate and emerge at different times. The regional voice will dominate in the early section as James vents his spleen at his sister, and it will recur when his wrath erupts again in chapter 5. But it will be, as we shall see, the more meditative voice that will dominate in the later sections where James comes to an accommodation with his sister, his friends, and the world.

Other Voices

Sally Page Abbot is, politically and culturally, her brother's opposite. She has, through her marriage to a cultivated dentist and her friendship with educated people, developed a perspective broader than her brother's. She favors amnesty for Vietnam War protestors, equal rights for minorities, and greater freedom for women. She and her husband had befriended Richard Page and abetted his courtship with an Irish Catholic girl whom James opposed.

Despite these differences, Sally is very much James's sister. She shares her brother's tragic sense and even comes upon his gravitational metaphor to express it: "feeling as if she were endlessly falling, sinking toward death, as if she'd somehow become conscious of the earth's fall through space" (227). More important, she shares her brother's obstinacy and his penchant for self-dramatization. She describes her quarrel with James as that between the oppressed and the oppressors of the world, and she stubbornly refuses to leave her room despite the pleas of her friends. Her high-minded liberalism has led her to dishonesty: she intercepts her brother's phone calls to prevent him from contributing to the Republican party or from hiring anyone who is not a black or a woman. When James learns of these acts, his fury erupts again, and their conflict reaches its most dangerous stage.

Their warfare will leave casualties in its wake: Ginny, James's daughter, will receive a head wound, and Ed Thomas, a family friend, will suffer a heart attack as a result of his efforts to mediate James and Sally's quarrel. Although trivial in its origins, this brother-sister dispute will have serious consequences in this little community. Who, finally, is to blame? James initiates the conflict, and Sally is correct to insist upon her rights. To give in to James would be simply to encourage his intolerance. Sally is, however, unnecessarily self-righteous and intransigent, and she must share responsibility for the injuries that result.

James and Sally are the central figures in the novel's conflict, but a range of other characters are drawn in and are instrumental in its resolution. Their reactions to James and Sally guide our reactions, and their attitudes suggest alternatives to the frozen postures that James and Sally have struck. Ginny, James's daughter, is the first to become involved. She is torn by conflicting loyalties and sees both the strengths and weaknesses of her father and her aunt's cases. At first glance, she seems ineffectual in her attempts to run her own life and to resolve her father's crisis. While it is true that she has her weaknesses—she is a chain-smoker who cannot keep house in an orderly fashion—it is also true that she is an attentive mother for her son and a loving daughter to James. In the final analysis, her patient concern proves crucial. She waits her father out, refusing to become angry herself; more important, she takes the blow meant for him and, in so doing, helps to waken the disputants to the consequences of their stubbornness.

Ginny's husband, Lewis, also contributes. James and Sally tend to patronize him because he is only a handyman with no fixed income. Lewis, however, has not chosen his profession out of indolence, but because it allows him to remain independent of other people's affairs. He chooses to stay out of his neighbors' quarrels because he sees the deep ambiguity of all moral questions. "Right and wrong," for Lewis, "were as elusive as odors in an old abandoned barn," thus "he could too easily see all sides and, more often than not, no hint of a solution" (124). Lewis does not involve himself directly in his in-laws' argument, but he is always in the near vicinity, working patiently at some practical task. His down-to-earth sobriety is a silent reproach to the surrounding excitement, and his quiet presence seems to dissipate some of the hysteria.

Ginny and Lewis contribute passively, but several of their friends take more active roles. Among these, Estelle Parks is particularly important. A retired high-school English teacher, Estelle benefits from a lifetime reading the world's best literature and a career working with people of all ages and types. She sympathizes with her friend Sally but sees that brother and sister are both "stubborn idealists" (208). She looks past the political issues to see a human problem to be solved in human terms. Her solution is to invite Sally and James's friends to a party at James's house in the hope that Sally and James will soften and join in. It does not work out as Estelle plans, but her gathering sets in motion the events—including the injury and the heart attack—that finally bring James and Sally to their senses.

Among Estelle's invitees is the Reverend Lane Walker, Sally's pastor. Walker engages Sally in conversation through her closed bedroom door, but the conversation takes a wrong turn when he makes a passing reference to apes, which Sally mistakes as an insult directed at her. This prompts a lengthy disquisition by Walker on apes, humans, and evolution. The burden of this disquisition is that the human species is continuing to evolve and that our tool-making capability effects that evolution; the direction of that evolution is, then, impossible to predict. The implication of these theses, which Walker leaves unstated and which no one in his hearing quite grasps, is that both James and Sally are mistaken. To defend their respective moral positions, James generalizes from the past and Sally generalizes from her vision of the future. For Walker, however, the human experience in time is far too fluid, ambiguous, and difficult to anticipate to allow such absolute judgments. Although Sally misses his point, Walker's sermon momentarily deflects her anger and calms it. He will intervene again late in the novel to effect James's reconciliation with a Mexican priest whom James has insulted. Walker, a civil-rights activist, shares many of Sally's liberal attitudes, but he does so with more tolerance than Sally manages. He is a practical, committed Christian with a sense of humor, and he represents a significant moral reference point in the novel.

The Unlocking of James Page

Among the others whom Estelle Parks brings to the Page farmhouse are Father Rafe Hernandez, a friend of Walker, and Ed and Ruth Thomas, a farmer and his librarian wife. They join in a party featuring songs and hot cocoa, but it is all brought to an end when James threatens Hernandez with his shotgun, triggering Ed Thomas's heart attack. Thomas plays a key role when James, now rather sheepish, visits him in the hospital. Ed has no bitterness for James; he has known of his heart condition and has accepted his imminent death. He and James are old friends, and they share many values. The men fall to reminiscing about political campaigns, and Ed points out how television has made them easier to follow—subtly suggesting that James has been mistaken about the medium he has so intemperately banned from his home.

Ed then talks of the changing seasons. As they sit talking in October, "locking time" is already beginning. The ground will freeze, and the days grow shorter. Then, after the winter solstice, another movement will begin. The sun will gradually reappear and shine more brightly on the snow, heralding the coming of "unlocking time," the beginnings of spring. Gradually, as the two farmers sit talking of the spring Ed will not live to see, the natural miracle they have been describing occurs within James. His heart had been locked; now without any direct discussion of it, it has been unlocked by his confrontation with his friend's approaching death and by their evocation of nature's mysterious rebirth. James walks out into the hospital waiting room where Lane Walker notices the change and subtly effects James's reconciliation with Father Hernandez.

James returns home and concedes to Sally. The unlocking continues.

Memories of his wife, deceased many years earlier, now surge into his mind. He reviews their life together and realizes "that life had been good once . . . and that life *was* good, as poor Ed Thomas understood now more clearly than ever, now that he was dying" (428). He remembers his son's death and finally confronts and accepts his own guilt:

Benighted, the lot of them, himself worst of all. He'd prayed for punishment, and had been punished well: punished years before the prayer.

Tears streamed down the old man's face, though what he felt did not even seem sorrow, seemed merely knowledge, knowledge of them all from inside, understanding of the waste. (430)

It is significant to note that this reconciliation occurs in the more sophisticated idiom of reflection that we discussed earlier. It is an idiom that now incorporates the language and judgments of others, for the crucial word "benighted" is borrowed from Lane Walker. It is in this more open idiom that James can manage the most crucial unlocking of all. James escapes his own limited point of view to achieve "knowledge of them all from inside": he can now sympathetically identify with those, like Richard, whom he previously had rejected. James then returns to the farm work—tending his beehives—that he interrupted earlier. Still caught in his memories, he suddenly realizes that an enormous black bear has approached, drawn by the honey. James raises his shotgun, aims it at the bear's head, but at the last moment he jerks his arm up and fires in the air. Later, James attempts to explain what happened to Lewis, and his explanation concludes the novel:

"And you didn't shoot at him?" Lewis said, looking thoughtfully past him with that one blue eye, one brown eye.

"I fahgot!" James said, squeezing his lower lip between his right-hand finger and thumb.

"It theemed like—" He broke off, realizing he must have, for an instant, fallen into a dream. It had seemed to the old man that the bear had said something, had said to him distinctly, reproachfully, *Oh James, James!* (434)

Once again Gardner ends his novel with a tantalizingly ambiguous scene. At the risk of simplifying this ambiguity, I would like to explore some of the meanings it suggests. The three principal elements—the gun, the bear, and the voice—all occur elsewhere in the novel, and those earlier occurrences resonate in this final tableau. The gun is the one with which James destroyed Sally's television and the one with which he menaced her and her friends. It is a symbol of his masculine drive to control and to enforce that control violently if necessary. His first, instinctive reaction is to use the gun as he had used it before, to destroy, but instead he uses it to scare the bear away and, in effect, to protect it.

The bear has come into James's consciousness several times before as a metaphor. The first instance is in the passage, quoted earlier, expressing his resolve not to give in to his sister: "let a bear live in the woodshed, he'd soon have your bed" (4). The bear here is the farmer's enemy—the natural brute that steals the fruit of honest human toil. James's moral absolutism can grant no place to such an animal. Later, however, in a different voice, he will use the metaphor to describe himself in his clumsy moral search. Here he remembers his anguished reaction to his son's suicide: he "had walked on the mountains at night, prowling like a lost bear hunting for the door to the underworld" (303; see also 14). The bear will take on one more meaning in the final confrontation at the beehive. James, in awe of the six-hundred-pound beast towering in front of him, remembers the rough heroes of the American Revolution: "Ethan Allen had been put upon the earth like Hercules, to show an impression of things beyond it. So it was with this enormous old bear that stood sniffing at the wind and studying him" (433). The bear thus, in the course of the novel, figures first as the enemy, then as James himself, and finally as a deeper reality glimpsed in the hero and in the majestic creations of nature.

The words James hears in this scene do not belong to the bear at all but to Ariah, James's wife. James has recalled them three times before, twice in close proximity to the image of himself as the bear (14, 304) and the third in proximity to the magic-door image associated with the bear (428). The words are Ariah's deathbed utterances to her husband, speaking his name, gently rebuking his stubbornness, and, at the same time, forgiving him with the wisdom that came to her facing death: "*Oh James, James!*"

Let us review what has happened to James Page in the final hours of the novel. He has spent his entire life fighting nature, not only outside—the rocky Vermont soil, the brutal winters—but inside—everything within him that might accede to the grave's downward pull. But the farmer does not only stand against nature but within it: the man and the bear—"the two ancient creatures" (433) staring at each other across the beehive—are brothers. The burden of Ed Thomas's gentle meditation on the seasons is that nature is good, trust it, give yourself to its eternal rhythms. The theme of James's rediscovered memories is that life is good, if one will only accept it on its own terms. Thus this final scene seems to suggest James's reconciliation with nature outside and within.

But this reconciliation is achieved not in isolation—the romantic hero alone in the forest—but in *society*. The voice speaking James's name is a human voice, and we hear in it not only Ariah, but all the others—Ginny, Lane Walker, Ed Thomas—who, with the same mixture of reproach and forgiveness, have patiently appealed to James's better nature. It is the love, patience, and tolerance of James and Sally's family and friends that gradually draw them back to moral and emotional health. As in the great comedies of the past, the natural and the social are linked: health can occur on one level only if there is health on the other level. But finally it is the social that receives primary emphasis in this bicentennial novel; in it Gardner explores the human values that underlie dialogue and democracy.

A Dialogue on Art

In addition to the dialogue on moral and social values within the narrative, there is also a dialogue on artistic values at the novel's metafictional level. As engrossing as the narrative is, we are continually reminded that we are reading a work of literary art. The text's literary status is called to our attention, first of all, by the elaborate use of titles and epigraphs for the chapters. These conventions had their origins in the serial publication of fiction in the eighteenth and nineteenth centuries, but they are little used today. When they are used—as in, for instance, John Barth's *The Sot-Weed Factor*—they have the effect of reminding us of the conventionality of literature and of the fact that we are reading a fiction. We are further reminded of the latter fact by the inclusion of a novel within the novel. Sally, a captive in her room, finds a pulp novel there and begins to read it to pass the time. As we read it over her shoulder, we inevitably confront our own status as readers of a fiction. This literary self-consciousness causes us to give special attention to moments in the novel where artistic issues are directly confronted.

The most obvious of these is Sally's reading of *The Smugglers of Lost Soul's Rock*. We should look closely at this reading because some critics have argued that its cynicism and violence significantly affect Sally's behavior. Confined with no other distractions, Sally begins a book she would not have considered reading in other circumstances. She initially finds it silly, but gradually she is drawn into its narrative. She sees similarities between the characters and her own family, and she takes satisfaction in the way the book seems to mock James's conservative and sexist values. She notes an increased cynicism on her own part and suspects that it is an "unhealthy effect" (38) of her reading. She continues, however, because she judges that she is not "some child, going to be corrupted by a foolish book" (54). Gradually, Sally becomes increasingly irritated by the novel. It touches on interesting ideas but fails to pursue them, and, in the case of a black female character, it seems to recommend a passivity that Sally rejects. Finally, the novel's plot becomes so boring and improbable that Sally loses all patience and angrily throws it against the wall.

The novel comes into Sally's possession because Dickey, Ginny's son, finds it in the pigpen where James had discarded it; Dickey then leaves it in the bedroom where Sally finds it. When Ginny is injured by an applecrate booby trap rigged by Sally for James, Dickey blames himself for the injury because he left the book in Sally's room. Several critics have taken the child's remark at face value: "It is *The Smugglers of Lost Soul's Rock* that urges Sally to violence and perversity—bad art pressing its influence upon life. Had the book remained where Gardner no doubt believes it belonged, the feud perhaps would have ended long ago, good sense prevailing. In his own simple and childlike way, Dickey states Gardner's own aesthetic position."[2]

Sally has retreated to her room because James has fired a shotgun at her television and has threatened her with a heavy wooden club. She stays there because James continues to menace her and because of a natural stubbornness formed long before she read the novel. She fixes the booby trap because James has earlier rigged a shotgun booby trap for her; more recently he has fired the gun above the heads of her friends and announced that Sally would be his next target. The box half full of apples is the nearest thing to a protective weapon that she can find in her room and the adjoining attic. Under the circumstances it is hard to imagine her acting differently, regardless of what she had read. During the planning and the setting of the trap, the book does not enter her consciousness. After it is set, she notes that the idea seemed to come to her from nowhere in the same way that a very different trap came to one of the novel's characters. When Dickey blames himself for his mother's injury, Lewis, ever the clear-headed

Yankee, answers commonsensically: "Your mother was hit by an applecrate. . . . It want your book" (360).

The *Smugglers of Lost Soul's Rock* is, nonetheless, an important component in the novel's artistic dialogue. Comprising nearly a third of
October Light, it forms a contrast with the novel surrounding it and sets
in relief the features of the latter, more significant fiction. Some critics,
noting this contrast, have tried to characterize it as immoral fiction
versus moral fiction. My own feeling is that such a characterization
gives *Smugglers* far more credit than it deserves. An immoral fiction,
presumably, espouses a deleterious ethical position that it subtly persuades its readers to adopt. To achieve this effect, the novel must do
two things. It must articulate a clear and coherent ideology, and it
must draw its readers under its spell, cause them to identify with its
characters and plot for a sustained period, such that the readers can be
influenced by that ideology. To my mind, *Smugglers* manages neither
of these tasks. Its ideas are fragmentary, when they are not murky or
contradictory; its plot is thoroughly implausible. Sally's exasperated
reaction—she finds the ideas "preachy" (377) and the plot "stupid"
(389)—proves these points.

To be fair, *Smugglers* does not ask to be taken as seriously as the
ethical vocabulary assumes. The names it gives its characters—Captain
Fist, Mr. Nit, Dr. Alkahest—freely acknowledge that they are
implausible caricatures. The self-consciously literary chapter titles—
"Alkahest Agonisties," "This Proves Ye Are Above, Ye Justicers"—
mock both the novel's actions and its intellectual pretensions. The
book's main purpose seems to be to amuse by combining topical references with sex, violence, and surprise. Its flip tone and its philo
sophical name-dropping suggest that it aims at a more sophisticated
audience than does most pulp fiction, but its fundamental purposes—
diversion, amusement, and momentary stimulation—remain the same.

Smugglers raises important issues, but it shows no interest in exploring them clearly or in detail. The most appropriate description, then,
is "unserious fiction," a term Gardner uses in *The Art of Fiction*.[3] *Smugglers'* main purpose in *October Light* is to contrast with the more serious—more authentically dialogical—fiction that encompasses it.
October Light's principal narrative introduces significant attitudes and
handles them responsibly by embodying them in characters who test
them in interaction with other characters and attitudes.

Another component in the artistic dialogue is the ideas contained in
the subchapter "Terence on Pure and Subservient Art." Terence Parks,

Estelle Parks's nephew, has attended the party organized by his aunt at
the Page farm and has witnessed the dramatic events that take place
there. The next morning Terence, a horn player, listens to a recording
of Tippett's "Sonata for Four Horns" on his parents' stereo. This experience causes him to reflect on the nature of music. There are, he
decides, two kinds: work music and real music. Work music is an
inferior form; it strives to describe a scene or a specific mood—program
music and ballet music are examples. Real music, on the other hand,
strives simply to be "its note-by-note self" (368). The Tippett sonata,
for instance, "meant nothing at all but what it was: panting, puffing,
comically hurrying French horns" (366). The young musician is thus
led to his own formulation of aesthetic purism.

Then a curious thing happens. Deeply immersed in the sonata,
Terence dreams he sees Richard Page, hanging dead from an attic raf-
ter: "In the dream—or perhaps inside Tippett's music—Terence had
stared at the faceless, still figure and had realized someone was in terrible danger, drifting out of key, out of orbit toward nothingness, toward emptiness and itself. *Margie?*, he wondered in brief panic. *Ed
Thomas? Aunt Estelle?* For a split second he understood everything,
life's monstrosity and beauty. Then he was listening to the horns again"
(369–70). Real music, it turns out, can do its own kind of "work,"
much deeper and more important than the programmatic evocation of
a set idea. By being, as purely as possible, its own musical self it can
sometimes, miraculously, trigger in us a profound understanding of
our own situation.

Terence's ideas and his experience help us to understand the aesthetic
at work in this novel. Fiction, because it uses words that carry deno-
tations, can never be pure in the same way that music can. Nonetheless, it best realizes its purpose of helping us to understand ourselves
and one another by, first of all, being itself: telling a story as honestly
and compellingly as possible. Unless it first succeeds as fiction, it cannot succeed at larger, illuminative purposes. Such illumination, moreover, comes as it will, out of the mysterious conjunction of personal
and literary experience, rather than from any predetermined didactic
program.

An additional voice in the artistic dialogue is supplied by an authorial excursus on the folk reciter. The digression occurs because Ruth
Thomas, a guest at the party, is a performer of this type. Such individuals, common in nineteenth-century rural America, entertain at
family and public gatherings by reciting popular verse. The narrator

approves of such art and explains that it can flourish "when no fine distinctions between bad and good are thought necessary, so that the more-or-less good has a way of prevailing, unthreatened by the over-reaching snatch at 'the Great' which creates failed masterworks and devalues the merely excellent, leaving all the world rubble and a babble of mixed-up languages" (262).

The issue of Ruth's poetry returns in her husband's hospital conversation with James Page. After his long evocation of nature's changing seasons, Ed asks James why he has bothered to listen to it. James can only answer that he has done so because it is true. Ed responds that this is the only way he and his wife can discriminate among poems: "only the good poems are exactly true" (418). James, for his part, compares the successful poem to a good window sash, his particular example for the well-crafted object, and Ed answers, "You got it" (418). The theme of the folk reciter and her poetry introduces into the novel a notion of art that is modest, well-made, and, especially, congruent with the experience of sensitive but ordinary Americans. It is a definition appropriate to *October Light* but not to *The Smugglers of Lost Soul's Rock.*

There is, I think, a certain convergence between the moral and artistic ideas explored in this novel. It is a work both ethically and aesthetically democratic: confident in the moral reasonableness and artistic taste of ordinary Americans. It is also a work that is willing to be modest and patient in pursuing its ethical and aesthetic purposes. Estelle Park's reflections on Lane Walker's sermons are pertinent here. She loves his homilies, such as the one on evolution he delivered outside Sally's bedroom door, but she is often puzzled by them: "He was fond of building up elaborate, merry structures of logic and Biblical or secular quotation—not so much sermons as prose poems, you might say—and ending with a sudden, quite striking allusion or an echo of something he'd said earlier, so that your heart leaped with pleasure, exactly as it would at some wonderful insight, but when you asked yourself just what it meant you had no idea" (232).

Gardner's "prose poems" are a bit like this. He leaves us with memorable characters, significant events, and arresting images—James and the bear at the beehive, for instance. But they cannot easily be reduced to a simple moral lesson. As we live with them and consider them more fully, however, they seem to resonate with deep and consequential meaning.

Chapter Nine
Freddy's Book

Freddy's Book (1980), one might argue, could more properly be titled *Jack Winesap's Book*. The novel has two distinct portions. The second and longest of these is a historical allegory written by a reclusive young giant named Freddy Agaard. The first portion is narrated by Jack Winesap, an historian who meets Freddy and his father while lecturing in Wisconsin. It is Winesap who meets Freddy and persuades him to share his composition with the world. Before Winesap, there was Freddy's *manuscript,* but it is only after Winesap, and through his intervention, that we have Freddy's *book.* That there is such a book is one of the key events of this novel.

Jack Winesap's Quest

I would like to discuss the novel's two sections separately in their order of presentation and then discuss the relationship between these sections. The first problem we confront in beginning Winesap's narrative is Winesap himself. He is, as I have suggested, crucial to the book's existence, and he is also the first section's narrator and principal actor. Who is he? The answer is complex because we form two different impressions as his narrative proceeds. The first is of an intellectual performer, a familiar type on the university lecture circuit. His professional colleagues may very well regard his work as facile and intellectually suspect, yet they will recommend him to their lectures committee because his presentations can be counted on to be lively and controversial. Our first impression is that Winesap is of this type. His lecture topic—"The Psychopolitics of the Late Welsh Fairy Tale: Fee, Fie, Foe—Revolution"—blends the pedantic and the trendy, and his parenthetical reminder in his second sentence that this article has been widely reprinted seems self-important.

This first impression, however, gradually gives way to a more sympathetic one. Winesap, to be sure, is a bit fatuous, but, to his credit, he knows this and even mocks himself good-humoredly. He feels sympathy for the overworked graduate students he meets, and he expresses affectionate concern for his wife and family. His lecture topic, despite its suspect methodology, shows sympathy for the underdog, in this instance, the Welsh in their struggle with the more powerful English. Jack Winesap, we gradually decide, is a decent sort, as well as a lively and trustworthy narrator.

But he is more than this, for Jack Winesap has several qualities that give him ethical ballast. There is, first of all, surprising moral sobriety; Winesap knows the hard truth about our condition. He "holds all effort to be at least partly vanity, a heroic, death-defying labor of bees making honey that will rot in a season."[1] In addition to this clearheaded realism, Winesap has another characteristic that is central to Gardner's moral view: openness to others. As he holds forth at the postlecture cocktail party, Winesap listens appreciatively to his interlocutors. Dialogue is crucial to his evolutionary concept of truth and its discovery: "I rather enjoy being proved—conclusively and cleanly—to be mistaken. It's Nature's way, I like to think: the Devonian fish corrected little by little through the ages into the milkcow, the gazelle, the princess with golden tresses who refills my glass" (5–6). Winesap's ability to listen, understand, and sympathize will prove crucial in the working out of the story he tells.

That story gets under way when he meets Sven Agaard, a distinguished but curmudgeonly medievalist, at the cocktail gathering. The conversation is rudely interrupted by Agaard's announcement that his son is a monster. The conversation then trails off in embarrassment. The next day, however, Winesap receives an invitation to visit Agaard. Agaard's meandering letter seems, on one hand, to plead for help and, on the other, to threaten an embarrassing scene if Winesap should be so brash as to accept. Winesap is puzzled as to how to read these mixed signals, but he finally decides to accept the anguished scholar's invitation. Winesap must continue to deal with ambiguity after he travels through a heavy blizzard to Agaard's home. This gloomy structure, seemingly designed by Monk Lewis, features all the gothic appurtenances: graveyard gate, cavewind drafts, and creaky doors. And yet the obligatory black cat is named Posey, and the otherwise forbidding Agaard brings out a surprisingly good wine for Winesap's enjoyment.

Winesap and Agaard's conversation moves by fits and starts until it strikes the topic of psychohistory. Agaard can now release his resentment at modern historians, psychohistorians in particular. Such scholars, Agaard argues, excuse themselves from the difficult work— mastering obscure languages, crawling through musty archives, carefully sifting facts—and yet they reap the benefits of attentive audiences, comfortable lecture fees, and remunerative publishing contracts. Worst of all, they distract themselves and others with trivial topics, such as fairy tales, that offer no moral substance. Agaard seems to get the best of this historical skirmish, since Winesap offers no refutation and acknowledges to himself Agaard's superiority as a practitioner of the traditional discipline.

But on the deeper epistemological and ethical issues that lie beneath their disagreement, Agaard is dead wrong. His veneration of "hard-won facts" and "incontrovertible proofs" (36) seems naive; Winesap knows that what seems apodictic at one moment in a given culture may only appear so because of that culture's hidden biases. History, rather than an impartial, exact science, is often "the tale of human struggle as it's told by the side that won" (33). Agaard, who seems unwilling to admit this subjectivity, misses the irony of his own concluding remark—"it's a fact, Winesap. Take my word for it!" (35)—but we should not.

Such epistemological naiveté has serious moral consequences, as Winesap realizes: "The trouble with incontrovertible proofs, I might have told him, is that they shut down conversation, inspire not mutual exploration through debate but scorn and attack. You prove that your man in his castle of logic and hard-won facts got some trivial detail wrong . . . , and as his knights come fleeing in dismay to your side—blushing, stammering, hitting themselves for shame—you blast his elegant fortress to Kingdom Come" (36). More is at stake here than a struggle over academic turf; the issue is the way we approach a humanistic discipline and, beyond that, the way we reach out to understand our fellow humans. This human concern remains paramount for Winesap throughout his visit. It is this that causes him to come, despite the risk of a professional attack, and it is this that causes him to not answer back when the attack is made. Agaard's mind will not be changed by Winesap's defense, and it might destroy what has become the visit's main purpose: to meet and to help Freddy.

Winesap realizes that purpose when Agaard leads him to Freddy's room. After recovering from his astonishment at the giant's size, he notes the boy's obvious ill health. He checks his initial anger at Agaard for allowing the condition to exist and generously concedes that he does not know all the difficulties with which Agaard has had to contend. Winesap comments on the mythical creatures that Freddy has modeled from tissue paper and balsa; Agaard's response—"Freddy doesn't make paper dragons anymore" (47)—in effect, deprecates the creations as the work of a child. Winesap, more sensitive, asks Freddy if their inspiration is Chinese, and Freddy answers that he worked from French illustrations. Agaard intervenes again to dismiss both the French and Freddy's work with a fatuous national stereotype:"It *looks* French! . . . It looks like it *ate* too much" (48).

Agaard mentions Freddy's writing, and Winesap follows on this, trying to establish common ground. Writing, he points out, is the great equalizer: each of us, despite other differences, faces the same fears and fatigues when we put pen to paper. Winesap knows that behind this effort, no matter how solitary, there is always a desire to contact others. He talks on, encouraging Freddy, but at the crucial moment he withdraws. He has made clear his interest in Freddy's writing if Freddy should wish to share it, but he also respects Freddy's right to refuse the offer and to protect his privacy. Later that evening he decides to reinforce their common bond as writers by giving Freddy the only copy of his talk; he guesses that Freddy may appreciate the paper's sympathy with the underdog. Later still, Freddy reciprocates. Winesap hears heavy footsteps in the night, watches his bedroom door open, and finds on the moonlit floor Freddy's manuscript.

Freddy's Manuscript: The Knight's Quest

This manuscript, the second half of this novel, is a historical allegory. Freddy sets his narrative in sixteenth-century Sweden, and he refers to numerous important figures in Sweden's struggle for independence from Denmark, most notably Gustav Vasa, later King Gustav I of Sweden. This was a time, Freddy's manuscript reminds us, from which our distinctively modern political and social arrangements emerged. Freddy's primary focus, however, is not political but moral; thus he allows himself techniques that no historian—not even the most audacious psychohistorian—would allow: Freddy introduces imaginary characters, mythic beings, and the supernatural into his allegory. His novella tells us how his imaginary hero, the giant Lars-Goren Berquist, managed to kill the devil.

Behind the allegorical drama lies a moral dialogue in which the principal participants are Lars-Goren and Bishop Hans Brask. The latter has been charged with protecting the Holy See's interests at a time when Scandinavia is being pulled apart by the Danish-Swedish rivalry and when Christendom is being divided by the Protestant Reformation. Brask began as an idealist, but the rivers of blood that he has seen flow for "good" causes have left him morally numb. So deep is his cynicism that Brask distrusts faith, rhetoric, and even language itself. Sensing the historical changes, the disillusioned cleric pragmatically joins Gustav Vasa's campaign to drive the Danes out of Sweden, a campaign that Lars-Goren has joined for more idealistic motives.

Brask does not mask his cynicism from his fellow conspirators, and he offers them a catechism in moral realism. For these purposes he sets up a schema that is geographical as well as moral. The northern, rural areas from which Lars-Goren has come contrast strikingly with the southern, urban courts of Stockholm, Copenhagen, and Rome, where Brask has had to work. Lars-Goren's native Halsingland is a kind of Eden, Brask argues, physically beautiful and morally pure, but unreal and doomed to disappear. Powerful new energies—increased trade, greater mobility, a surging merchant class—are reshaping the geographical and moral map, creating urban agglomerations where the law of the jungle prevails. "Who can help growing greedy and corrupt, in places like that?" the bishop asks, "Cheat or be cheated, that's the rule" (215). In Brask's schema, the countryside permits a moral naiveté that is more appropriate to an animal or a child, while the city requires the moral sophistication of an adult. Several characters in the narrative seem to confirm Brask's analysis. Father Karl, a priest whom Lars-Goren meets on his return home, embodies the simple-minded moral code that Brask attributes to country folk. For this rural pastor, all evil is the devil's work; the peasants are not to be blamed. Such naive faith may be comforting, but Gustav Vasa, who begins idealistically, discovers that, once he enters the urban power centers, he must embrace Brask's pragmatism.

Brask's schema, if we take it at face value, confronts us with a dilemma. Father Karl's simple piety is clearly inadequate. And yet the strongest argument against Brask's position is Brask himself, for the bishop's cynicism has led to philosophical confusion and moral impotence. He doubts the value of all human acts and cannot even put pen to paper to write his own story, an account that, in another part of his mind, he wants desperately to write. To his credit, we glimpse in this frustrated desire some hope that he still believes in the possibility of truth. We catch another hint of a different Brask in an early scene. Brask poses before Lars-Goren and Gustav Vasa as a morally indifferent aesthete, a kind of medieval Des Esseintes. There are no moral criteria, only aesthetic ones; one lives only for style: "Always the intolerable

burden of style! Always the cool eye drifting toward the murder!—
excuse me, I meant *mirror!*" (111). Brask flushes at the slip and hur-
riedly withdraws, but we note that, at some deep level, he is morally
troubled by the crimes to which he has given assent. It is the presence
of this other level within Brask that accounts for his decision to join
Lars-Goren's idealistic journey to meet and kill the devil.

The most important objection to Brask's schema, I believe, is that
it is geographically and morally incomplete. If the north, the rural,
and the natural represent one terminus of this spectrum, that terminus
cannot be Lars-Goren's Halsingland, for there is one place in the narrative that is farther north, less inhabited, and less civilized. That place
is Lappland. The Lapps, who figure in the story's background and who
participate in its denouement, would seem to be nature's true primi-
tives. So completely have their lives become intertwined with that of
the reindeer upon whom they depend for food and clothing that they
seem simply a two-legged, hornless variant of that species. They
ought, if we follow Brask's geographical logic, to be philosophical sim-
pletons. It is true, Lars-Goren realizes, that living in a white wilder-
ness cuts the Lapps off from many things, but it also puts them in
contact with others; the Lapps live "in tune with the wind and snow,
the heartbeat of the reindeer, the mind of God" (238).

The Lapp worldview, as we learn it here, is simple but not simple-
minded. It accepts a spiritual reality that is neither benign nor malevo-
lent. "It was simply there, beneficial or harmful in about the way
wolves or reindeer are, a parallel existence neither loving nor malicious,
nor even consciously indifferent; a force to be reckoned with, avoided
or made use of, like the ghosts in one's hut of stretched hides" (83). It
also shows a profound awareness of evil. Indeed, a fact inconvenient to
Brask's north-south, innocence-experience schema is the belief that the
devil traditionally made his home not in the southern cities but in the
far north, in Lappland. Despite this awareness of evil, the Lapps have
not become morally impotent or cynical. Although they are not as
innocent as we might suppose, the Lapps do differ from Brask in one
important respect: they are intuitive while he trusts only reason. They
are preliterate—we might almost say preverbal, since they scarcely
speak—while Brask has seen the coming of the printing press. Blinded
by the brilliance of the new book culture, Brask misses the special,
instinctive genius of older, nonliterate cultures.

Our adjustment of Brask's moral map allows us to place Lars-Goren
Berquist. This knight occupies a place somewhere between the prim-

itive Lapps and the sophisticated bishop. He descends from Lapps through one of his grandmothers; he accepts, "below reason, their premise, a world of spirit" (83), and he enjoys premonitory glimpses of a spirit world. On the other hand, like Brask, he has known the responsibility of power and has had to face the poignant paradox that cripples Brask: he knows that doing good often requires doing evil and that helping some often means hurting others. He is made keenly aware of the latter fact when he returns home to confront the family he has had to leave because of his military duties. He meets in his son's eyes the reproach of one who has felt abandoned by his father. That reproach and his own feelings of guilt stay with him until later that night when, for the first time in several years, he takes his wife in his arms: "The feeling of strangeness and guilt fell away; he understood by sure signs that, odd as it might seem, he was the joy of her life, as she was of his" (129–30).

Lars-Goren discovers in this moment of intimacy the values by which he acts and which justify all that he has done. He knows that he has left his family and has gone to war to protect them and others for whom he is responsible. This instinctive, prerational love for those closest to one's self provides Lars-Goren's moral footing and protects him from the intellectual quicksand into which Bishop Brask has strayed. This love will continue to direct and protect the knight at the crucial moments of his quest.

We, and Lars-Goren, come to understand the particular resolve this quest requires when the knight views Bernt Notke's statue of Saint George killing the dragon. Lars-Goren discovers in the face of this elaborately carved wooden sculpture something he has not seen or understood before.

What he saw was the blank, staring face of the knight, gazing straight forward, motionless, as if indifferent to the monster, gazing as if mad or entranced or blind, infinitely gentle, infinitely sorrowful, beyond all human pain. I am Sweden, he seemed to say—or something more than Sweden. *I am humanity, living and dead.* For it did not seem to Lars-Goren that the monster below the belly of the violently trembling horse could be described as, simply, "foreigners," as the common interpretation maintained. It was evil itself; death, oblivion, every conceivable form of human loss. The knight, killing the dragon, showed no faintest trace of pleasure, much less pride—not even interest. (147–48)

Lars-Goren reads the statue morally, and it provides a commentary on the task he will soon set for himself. Saint George kills evil. His face reveals, however, a tragic awareness that this killing is itself evil, although necessary. The staring eyes seem also to see that such a victory can only be partial—the elimination of one incarnation of evil—and perhaps in the long run even futile. Despite this awareness, Saint George acts. He acts, however, with an extraordinary emotional control that protects him from any momentary distraction—the reproach in a son's eyes, for example—that might deflect him from his serious purpose. We will see this look again, for it is an important leitmotiv in Lars-Goren's story.

In addition to his deeply grounded moral resolve, Lars-Goren also embodies a commitment to dialogue. Brask sees in the knight an "openness of heart," an ethic that sees "evil as the closing of the heart, a refusal to communicate" (217). Although Brask mocks this ethic, the narrative provides two confirmations, one negative and one positive, of its value. Lars-Goren meets the ghost of a woman he has allowed to be burned for witchcraft. She was, she insists, innocent, and she rebukes him for never having allowed her to present her own case. Lars-Goren's son Erik seconds the reproach, and the knight acknowledges the tragic consequences of his failure to follow his ethic of openness. There is also positive proof of this ethic's value in the example of Brask, who is finally cured by it. The bishop, against all his precepts, accompanies the knight on his quest to kill the devil. He continues to mock the knight's moral resolve, but he also tells the story of his own lost ideals. Lars-Goren listens tolerantly and manages to understand and even sympathize with his opposite. His patience calms the bishop, and his courage seems to inspire him. In the final confrontation the bishop will be at the knight's side, and he will give his life assisting him.

It is time now to look at that confrontation and the novel's conclusion. It is a conclusion that is played out simultaneously in four separate locations, ranging across the geographical and moral map: two locations in Lappland and locations in Halsingland and Stockholm. These four separate actions alternate in the novel's last chapter. In one of these actions a Lapp magician taps a drumhead with three stones representing Lars-Goren, Brask, and the devil. At a crucial moment the grey stone representing Lars-Goren leaps forward; at the same instant elsewhere, Lars-Goren grips the reindeer-bone knife with which he will kill the devil. Back in Halsingland, the witch's ghost visits the knight's wife and informs her of her husband's action. The ghost seems reconciled and strangely proud of the knight's victory.

The principal action is, however, the final face-off between the two humans and the devil. The night before the confrontation the devil visits Lars-Goren in a dream and tries to dissuade him, first by sophistry, then by bribery. The knight awakens, reflects, and is held steady by the love of family we discussed earlier: "he was seeing his family in his mind's eye, and rational or not, he was thinking he must make the world safe for them" (235). He follows his Lapp guides to the devil's dwelling, and, as he does so, he notes how the Lapps "seemed to look at nothing and everything at once. . . . It was a look he had seen before somewhere" (241). The knight does not have time to identify the gaze, but we do: it is Saint George's seemingly unfocused but resolutely determined expression. We will see it again shortly thereafter. The bishop distracts the devil, and Lars-Goren plunges home his reindeer-bone knife. The devil, turning his head to see who has distracted him, discovers that "it was as if the man's mind had gone as blank as the face of Bernt Notke's carved statue . . . a face more empty of emotion than the face of the world's first carved-stone god" (245). Hans Brask in this final moment has, against all conscious intention, reached the deeper moral vision that sees all the worst truths about our world and yet remains capable of acting.

The fourth action in this parallel sequence occurs in Stockholm. King Gustav is about to sign a decree putting all his enemies to the sword. In the novel's last paragraph, after Lars-Goren has killed the devil, he suddenly changes his mind and resolves to use his parliament and his newly created press to subject the question to democratic discussion and resolution.

How do we read the tale's final sequence of events? What died here, and what is being born? Lars-Goren has killed the devil—maybe only *a* devil—but he has not killed evil. We know that humanity's capacity to rob, destroy, and murder for "noble" purposes has, if anything, increased since the sixteenth century, and the novel's penultimate chapter shows us the Muscovite czar moving to exploit the vacuum left by the destruction of the Danish empire. Who then is the devil who dies at the end of Freddy's story? He is indefatigably active—whispering in Swedish, Danish, German, and Italian ears—and yet of himself he does little. He is, in this, very like his opposite: "God's hands," Lars-Goren's son guesses, "are tied" (135). Neither the devil nor God controls human destiny, humans do; the devil works through them.

The entity that dies in the northern snows, I believe, is a certain notion of evil. That notion, which survived among a few witch-burners but which was already dying elsewhere, held that transcendental spiritual forces control human fate. The sixteenth century was discovering the sad but very modern truth that humans must accept responsibility for the good and evil they do. Whether the knight's victory, and the new awareness it symbolizes, was, in fact, a triumph is very much in doubt. Surely the story's final lines, which describe this new world, are far from triumphant in tone: "And now, like wings spreading, darkness fell. There was no light anywhere, except for the yellow light of cities" (246). We dwell more than ever, it seems, in the moral world of Bishop Hans Brask. And yet this tale seems to suggest that the example of Lars-Goren Berquist at this era's birth is still valid at this later stage of its development. Doubt and despair must be met and their causes honestly faced. But, having done so, grounds for moral confidence and for positive action can be found if we will only trust our age-old but still valid moral instincts.

The Dialogue Between the Narratives

Having looked at both Winesap and Freddy's stories we must ask how they come together in this novel. Their relationship is, initially at least, obscure and troubling, for the first story is longer, its characters more developed, and its themes more consequential than most prefaces; we are left wanting to know more. And yet it does not seem to be a conventional frame tale, for there is no completing portion to this frame. How do the two halves of this novel function, and how do they result in a literary experience that is more resonant than the reading of two separate and unrelated narratives? We can, I think, approach the question in two ways: we can see the two stories sequentially as linked units in a single narrative, and we can listen to them as two separate voices in a dialogue. To begin with the narrative approach, we note that the author of the second story is one of the three characters in the first. Thus the presentation of this second narrative is an act of communication between its author and these two other characters.

The silent sliding of the manuscript across the moonlit floor to Jack Winesap is, first of all, a reaching out to Winesap. Winesap has argued that every instance of putting pen to paper is, implicitly at least, a desire to communicate. Freddy now makes this desire explicit, and he accepts the risks of misunderstanding, ridicule, and rejection that

Winesap earlier assumed in his parallel gesture to Freddy. It is also a reaching out to Agaard. We must remember that Freddy shares responsibility for his isolation. It is Freddy who has put the bars on his windows and the locks on his drawers, and it is Freddy who has refused to acknowledge the existence of a manuscript to his father. He must know that, in the absence of any explicit contrary instructions, Winesap will share it with Agaard.

The sharing with his father requires greater courage—because it runs greater risks—than the sharing with Winesap. His manuscript itself is both an homage and an act of rebellion against the elder Agaard. It is, after all, set in medieval Sweden, the area in which his father has established himself as an eminent authority. Following in his father's footsteps, is, in a sense, a tribute to his parent. But Freddy uses techniques distinctly different from those approved by the senior historian. Freddy is not writing history, and he must hope that his father will be open-minded enough to grant other ways of discussing the world. I see in Freddy's act a plucky willingness to trust his father's basic fairness and generosity.

Freddy's manuscript is a text that inevitably reveals its author's concerns. His protagonist is, like Freddy, a giant. But size is relative, and there is at least one individual larger than Lars-Goren and one individual of whom he is terrified: the devil. The knight conquers his fear and, in the tale's climax, kills his devil. Freddy, more than his hero, is a frightened giant. Winesap shrewdly guesses that the individual who most terrifies Freddy—his personal "flesh-eating giant" (55)—is, paradoxically, the diminutive Agaard. If we have correctly interpreted Freddy's final gesture, he, like his hero, conquers his fear and lays his demon to rest. In considering Freddy's situation, we are inevitably reminded of Gardner's other "monster," Grendel. Monsterhood, in both instances, begins when society judges that an individual exceeds its physical norms and casts that individual out. Such an individual, if this taboo is enforced too rigidly, can become a moral monster, seeking violent revenge for his condition. Freddy, it seems, will escape this fate, for he has been offered the grace—the "someone to talk to"—refused to Grendel, and he has accepted it.

We discover another of Freddy's concerns when we recall that Lars-Goren is a father who has become estranged from his son. When Erik Berquist, resentful of his father's absence, reproaches his father for burning the witch, Lars-Goren threatens to disinherit him. Later, however, the knight's anger cools, and his respect for his son grows. Erik

will be allowed to rule Halsingland, and Lars-Goren's love for him will
be one of the forces that sustains him in the final battle. We do not
know if Freddy and Sven Agaard will be reconciled as fully as Erik and
Lars-Goren Berquist, but if our interpretation of his gesture is correct,
Freddy has taken the first step. Although Freddy could not consciously
have intended it as such, his tale turns out to have been a vicarious
rehearsal of the events following Winesap's overture.

In addition to discussing the two stories as parts of a single narrative, we can also hear them as two voices in a single dialogue within
the book. This dialogue is not the conflict of contrasting opinions seen
elsewhere but rather voices echoing complementary variants on the
same themes. Despite differences in settings and styles, the two stories
share common situations and ideas. In both stories the protagonists
effect significant changes; in one instance, the knight kills the devil
and opens the way to the modern era; in the other, the visiting historian allays Freddy's fears and opens his door to the outside world. Both
protagonists are clearheaded realists who nonetheless retain their abilities to act. This comparison helps us to see another theme in their
lives that we might otherwise miss. In both instances, the men's moral
resolve is assured by the love between father and son or between son
and father. It is his son's face that Lars-Goren sees when, after the
devil's temptation, he asks himself why he persists. Winesap, on the
night of the offering to Freddy, thinks several times of his son and of
his father. Here are his thoughts in the crucial moments between his
gift to Freddy and Freddy's reciprocal offering: "I remembered how my
father would look up smiling in the hayloft when he saw me coming
cautiously through the twilight with his supper—I was five or six—
and how he'd cry out 'Applejack!' his name for me . . . and he'd open
his arms to me, huge, thick farmer-arms, power itself. He'd been dead
for ten years now. I heard another sound, the sigh of another floorboard
as the giant's foot weighed on it. *It's only Freddy*" (63). The theme of
paternal and filial love is only suggested in the first story, but it echoes
more resonantly in the second. Taken together they suggest that the
age-old emotional ties between parent and child are an example of at
least one moral constant by which we can still set our ethical compass.

I would like at the end of this discussion of *Freddy's Book* to come
back to the character whose name—deliberately, I think—is not in the
book's title. It is Jack Winesap who has the last "word" here. He has
it by *not* speaking, by not coming back, as we might expect, to close
his frame. This action is characteristic and revealing. The ethic of

openness requires a generous acceptance of the other, a willingness to hear and respect another human being's particular view of the world. Winesap practices this ethic once more in his demure withdrawal. Freddy's tale is fully legitimate and autonomous, and it requires no seconding by Winesap. It is, as Winesap tells us, in his final words, "mysteriously still and sufficient on the dusty gray carpet—Freddy's book" (64).

Chapter Ten
Mickelsson's Ghosts

In the last novel published before his death, John Gardner chose, as he did in his first novel, a professional philosopher as his protagonist. Both *Resurrection*'s James Chandler and *Mickelsson's Ghosts*'s Peter Mickelsson are professors of philosophy who suffer through personal and professional crises. Chandler discovers that he has an incurable disease, and Mickelsson is caught in a painful divorce and several disruptive love affairs; in both cases the men will be forced to review their lives and their personal philosophies. Although Mickelsson does not face death, his crisis is, in some ways, more painful and more difficult to solve than Chandler's. Chandler's death sentence draws a line between him and his past and provides him with a certain objectivity from which to review it. He withdraws into the quiet of his hospital room to conduct that review in relative peace. Mickelsson's problem is not death but life or, more specifically, the vital but convulsive drives in his life that have destroyed his personal and professional tranquility. The issue, for Mickelsson as for Chandler, is rebirth: can an individual take responsibility for a life gone bad and change it? In Mickelsson's case, the answer is problematic precisely because he remains part of that life and captive to its pressures.

A Philosopher's Moral Crisis

Although their narrative situations are similar, the novels differ in their structures. In *Resurrection* the story is told through the consciousnesses of a half dozen different characters who witness Chandler's final days and whose responses create a dialogue on the issues his death poses. In *Mickelsson's Ghosts* (1982) the narration is restricted to the protagonist's point of view. The novel creates a dialogue no less rich, however, by the use of "ghosts," voices within Peter Mickelsson who represent different aspects of his disintegrating personality and of our disintegrating cultural tradition. Mickelsson has second sight, and thus these ghosts are, in some instances, apparitions of dead human beings. Mickelsson also, however, fantasizes conversations with colleagues, friends, and even famous thinkers of the past, and these voices are heard echoing through his consciousness.

The Mickelsson whom we meet at the novel's outset, sweltering in his underwear in a cheap apartment, faces a profound personal crisis. His twenty-year marriage has ended in an angry divorce, precipitating ruinous alimony payments and an Internal Revenue Service suit. His professional life is a shambles. He has had to leave a prestigious Ivy League university for a younger state institution, and he now misses classes, skips meetings, and allows his mail to accumulate unanswered on his cluttered desk. His personal life is even more anarchic. He cannot break the cycles of heavy drinking followed by hangovers and of casual sex followed by guilt and self-loathing. As with Agathon, another of Gardner philosophers, this self-loathing leads to a deep despair. He has lost faith with the whole philosophical enterprise, and he now inveighs intemperately against feminists and moderates, Germans and French, Marxists and conservatives. Virtually everyone and everything is unredeemed "pigshit."[1]

Mickelsson's fall into despair is all the more poignant in that he is a moral philosopher whose earlier life had been remarkable for its order, discipline, and tolerant reasonableness. The main thrust of his philosophical work was to base ethical theory on biology. According to Mickelsson, certain forms of behavior—self-sacrifice for the community, tolerance to opposing points of view—are crucial to the species's survival. Thus the evolutionary process has, in effect, programmed us with a propensity for these behaviors. Mickelsson attempted, in this fashion, to explain and justify biologically "the immediate human sense of life's sacred quality" (78), which traditionally had been supported by religious arguments. It is this nearly religious sense of life's sacredness that causes Mickelsson, in a graduate seminar, to argue against abortion. The tension between the earlier Mickelsson and his present self is dramatically revealed in one of the novel's early events. Mickelsson carries an antique carved walking stick, which he earlier selected as a relic of "the age when possessions were adornments of a life presumed-until-proven-otherwise to be noble and worthwhile" (7). Now, in a sudden and uncontrollable act of frustrated rage, he uses this beautiful walking stick to cruelly and unnecessarily crush the head of a dog.

Mickelsson is appalled by the person he has become and seeks to change by leaving the campus community and the distractions, temptations, and frustrations it represents. He sets out to explore the surrounding countryside, and, although the distance he travels from Binghamton, New York, to the Endless Hills of Pennsylvania is only forty miles, it soon becomes clear that the flight Mickelsson is attempting is to a much more distant time and place. As he moves beneath the crisp autumn sunshine, he is visited by memories of his Wisconsin childhood and exhilarated by the hope of rebirth. Two successive recollections suggest the nature of the rebirth he desires. He first remembers himself "running naked, as a boy, in his father's overgrown apple orchard, given over, by the time of his memory, to cows—running naked, his clothes and glasses hidden in the shadow of a tree, imagining as he ran the nakedness of his tall older cousin Mary Ann, or some naked female stranger from beyond the marsh" (20). The middle-aged philosopher, racked by the consequences of a failed marriage and casual, loveless affairs, dreams of a return to sexual innocence, a time when the body and its pleasures could be enjoyed without guilt.

He also recalls his grandfather, a Lutheran minister, and this memory introduces another theme in the nostalgia. He recalls the old man "in his dark, plain suit, sitting stiffly upright at his desk in the manse, books laid out in front of him, dusty late-afternoon sunlight slanting in, his steel-rimmed spectacles insensibly cutting red wounds into the sides of his peculiar, leftward-aiming nose" (20). The old clergyman, confident in his religious faith and unmindful of his body's weakness, represents an ideal of intellectual conviction and disciplined scholarship. The appeal of this image to his grandson, torn by intellectual doubts and convulsed by his appetites, is understandably powerful. Taken together, the images of the boy and the older pastor suggest the possibility of a return to sexual and intellectual innocence in a pastoral world. Unfortunately, these hopes will be cruelly disappointed, for moral change requires more than change of residence. Mickelsson, had he been less intoxicated with his pastoral dream, might also have noted that the two images he entertains here are in fundamental opposition. The stern Lutheran, he will recall later, had the nude portraits of Adam and Eve removed from his church.

Mickelsson's withdrawal into the country proves decisive in his life, but in ways he has not anticipated. The land he buys proves to be polluted chemically by toxic wastes. Even more important, it has been polluted morally by a succession of witches, religious fanatics, and murderers whose moral influence can still be felt on the property. Isolated in this strange environment, Mickelsson becomes even more dissolute in his behavior. To pay for his move, he raids a bank account he had set aside for his mother, and, when this proves insufficient, he writes bad checks and runs up credit accounts he knows he will not be able to repay. He pulls away from his university friends and refuses assistance to Michael Nugent, his student, and Jessica Stark, his colleague and lover, when they desperately need him. He also patronizes an uninhibited young prostitute in an affair that is a cruel parody of the sexual innocence he earlier fantasized. When this young woman, Donnie Mathews, becomes pregnant, Mickelsson plans to finance the child's birth by robbing and killing a former bank robber. The victim dies of a heart attack during the robbery, so Mickelsson is guilty of manslaughter rather than murder. Donnie uses the money for an abortion, an act that Mickelsson opposed and that the money was supposed to prevent. Mickelsson's pastoral flight, rather than solving his moral problems, has made them worse.

Ghostly Voices

The same is true for his emotional and intellectual struggles. Alone in the country on long winter nights, stimulated by alcohol and guilt, Mickelsson engages in lengthy and punishing self-examinations. His feelings of guilt make themselves felt in his encounters with apparitions. These ghosts—Caleb and Theodosia Sprague, a brother and sister who formerly inhabited Mickelsson's farmhouse—have been seen by others in the community, but they seem especially drawn to Mickelsson and become an almost constant presence in the farmhouse, particularly after his robbery and the death of his victim. Mickelsson is also drawn to them, deliberately conjuring their presence and seeking to piece together their story. Like Mickelsson, the mysterious Spragues withdrew to their farm to escape the outside world. Mickelsson learns from neighbors that Theodosia Sprague murdered her brother Caleb on the farm and was executed for that crime. He sees the two of them and a child in the house during his waking hours, but the crucial scene that enables him to reconstruct their story comes to him in a dream.

The dream environment allows his own conflicted feelings to surface, and the version that he creates seems as much a product of his own feelings as of the objective facts of the Sprague case. Mickelsson decides in the dream that the Spragues were incestuous lovers, and that Theodosia bore their child, the child that Mickelsson had seen earlier. They raised the child in secret until Caleb, driven by guilt, killed it.

In the dream, Mickelsson looks into a mirror where he discovers, not his own face, but Caleb's. He then watches Theodosia shoot Caleb to punish his murder of their child, and he sees Caleb's dying face become that of the fat man whom Mickelsson robbed and killed.

Mickelsson's dream and his version of the Sprague tragedy echo recent events in his own life. His affair with Donnie Mathews is not incestuous but is, in his own judgment, "lubricious and lewd, meretricious, debauched, profligate and goatish" (338). It also produces an illegitimate child. The Caleb and Theodosia of Mickelsson's dream reflect his conflicting reactions to this pregnancy and its consequences. Mickelsson, like Caleb, is a child-killer, for he finances Donnie's abortion. In another, more ethical, part of his personality, he repudiates this act and, like Theodosia, punishes the killer. The child victim of the dream represents both Donnie's fetus and the childlike innocence that Mickelsson had hoped to recover but that his recent actions have destroyed. The fat man of the dream is linked to both Caleb and Mickelsson because his money has made the abortion possible. The fat man also mirrors Mickelsson's feelings about his undisciplined appetites, which resulted in the pregnancy and which have turned his once athletic body into soft flab.

Cultural Voices

Mickelsson's interpretation of the Sprague tragedy represents only one way in which his internal struggle is dramatized. In addition to the second sight that enables him to see spirits, Mickelsson also enjoys a lively imagination and the capacity to see problems from points of view other than his own. Because of this he cannot really escape the community he has fled, for he carries its members' voices within him, and, during his four-month isolation, he will carry on internal dialogues with many of them. He discusses religion and philosophy with undergraduates, continues professional disagreements with his colleagues, argues tax matters with his attorney, and debates his mental health with his psychiatrist—all of this in his mind, with Mickelsson performing all of the parts. Even more important for the working out of his intellectual crisis are Mickelsson's imagined interactions with religious and philosophical figures from the past. In his nostalgia for the world represented by his grandfather, Mickelsson begins to read the writings of Martin Luther and his grandfather's commentaries on them. After these readings he imagines confessing his sins to Luther.

The confession brings little solace, however, for Mickelsson notes that Luther is sexually aroused by the sinner's account of his sins. Mickelsson here is influenced by his reading of Luther's own texts, which reveal powerful sexual urges and equally powerful guilt feelings. As with Mickelsson, these guilt feelings express themselves in a continual recourse to excremental imagery. In his inability either to rid himself of his sexual urges or to accept them without guilt, the Renaissance reformer appears strikingly similar to his modern student. During these studies, Mickelsson imagines he sees Luther in town, but it is, in fact, the fat man whom he eventually robs. In this way, the religious figure comes to represent not salvation but an intensification of Mickelsson's own guilt.

Mickelsson's philosophical speculations also include Friedrich Nietzsche, upon whom Mickelsson wrote his dissertation. Mickelsson regards Nietzsche's revolt against Luther as the central event in modern moral philosophy, and the German philosopher's words continually echo in his consciousness. Nietzsche, who like Mickelsson descended from a Lutheran clergyman, sought to push past Luther by announcing the death of God and the death of guilt-inducing Christian morality. He proclaimed "something nobler: the serene, spiritually mighty *Übermensch*" (402), a moral superman who would boldly step beyond conventional ethics to act on his own impulses. Encouraged by these Nietzschean reflections, Mickelsson decides to steal the fat man's money and soon carries out his plan. After doing so, however, and after having tried to live with the consequences, he views Nietzsche differently. He sees the German philosopher as a cowardly hunchback, obscenely worshiping the fierce Prussian soldier whom he could not emulate personally. Thus Mickelsson's Nietzschean leap proves as fruitless as his Lutheran confession.

One of Nietzsche's philosophical heirs, Ludwig Wittgenstein, is more helpful. Wittgenstein argued that metaphysical questions, such as the existence of God, are finally unanswerable and ought to be abandoned so that we can get on with the more concrete business of living. Wittgenstein is not personified in Mickelsson's consciousness as were Luther and Nietzsche, but Mickelsson continually hears his voice uttering the gnomic aphorisms of the *Tractatus*. Among these, Wittgenstein's phrase "the solution of the problem of life is seen in the vanishing of the problem" (480,499) is particularly important. It is in the spirit of Wittgenstein's teaching that Mickelsson decides that the true supermen were not Nietzsche's militarists but "men, who . . .

had given up thought long ago: men who simply acted—not out of pity but with infallible faith and love" (476). Mickelsson sees as an instance of this ideal his own father, a Wisconsin farmer who, unconcerned by religious or philosophical questions, lived in simple harmony with his family, friends, and nature. Mickelsson has emulated his father in his return to the farm, and he takes special pleasure in the way his hands, after hours of rough labor restoring his farmhouse, begin to resemble those of his parent. He must, however, admit a sad and important difference: his father did such work to provide shelter for the family he loved, but Mickelsson does his work "for the sake of no one" (476). This recognition anticipates Mickelsson's eventual decision to return to the human community.

The Solution to a Mystery

The novel's climax arrives with the solution of a series of crimes occurring in the area. Professor Warren has been murdered, and his murder is followed by the mysterious deaths of two of his students. Mickelsson's house is ransacked as is the house of Tom Sprague, Mickelsson's neighbor. Sprague is brutally murdered shortly thereafter. A number of rumors circulate regarding the students' homosexuality, Sprague's witchcraft, and a lawsuit between Sprague and the former owner of Mickelsson's farm. There is also speculation about homosexual motorcycle gangs, an IRS investigation, and mysterious Mafia activity. None of this has anything to do with the mystery's real culprit, who turns out to be Professor Edward Lawler.

Lawler previously has been glimpsed only at the novel's periphery. He is the philosophical colleague whom Mickelsson most admires: a brilliant Aquinas scholar, a master of languages, and a dedicated teacher. Lawler's disciplined pursuit of truth seems an implicit reproach to Mickelsson's indolence and intellectual vacillation. But, in the novel's final pages, Lawler turns out to be a member of a secret Mormon commando group, the Sons of Dan. He has imagined that Professor Warren, a Mormon apostate, is searching documents that might compromise the Mormon faith, and so he has murdered him. The precise nature of these documents and their threat to Mormonism are never explained. Warren was, in fact, investigating illegal toxic waste disposal. Lawler, not knowing this, also kills two students whom he believes Warren has told of the documents. Hoping to find the documents, he ransacks the Sprague and Mickelsson farms and kills

Sprague. Now, near the novel's end, he visits Mickelsson and forces him to tear apart his house in pursuit of the nonexistent documents. These developments are the novel's biggest weakness. The mystery story tradition, upon which the novel builds at this point, requires that the solution to the crime come as a surprise. It also insists that the solution he prepared by a system of incriminating clues so that the solution seems logically motivated by the plot. In this instance, Lawler is abruptly thrust to center stage with little preparation and declared the arch villain. The character himself strains credulity: it is difficult to believe that a man could lead two such radically different lives and that a man of Lawler's intelligence could launch himself on such a pointless, mistaken, and brutal mission. Lawler attempts to explain his motives as they search. He proclaims himself a religious cynic— "all religions are fraudulent at the foundation" (545); and yet he claims to believe with all his heart and mind in the teachings of the Mormon prophet Joseph Smith. Both Mickelsson and the investigating police doubt that Lawler was, in fact, a Son of Dan, or that such a group even exists. Was Lawler then simply an isolated madman? We are never told.

Mad or sane, Lawler does work from a clear intellectual position. He argues that most humans are fools who must be controlled by an intellectual elite; the elite alone is privileged to know the truth. For this modern Grand Inquisitor, the Mormon Church is the intellectual vanguard's vehicle for controlling the masses. These arguments hark back to issues raised by Mickelsson in his undergraduate philosophy class, issues that obviously preoccupy him in his current intellectual crisis. Is there, he asks, something inherently dangerous in the pursuit of transcendent ideas? Does not the belief that these mysterious truths can be grasped only by a gifted minority open a gap in society that will eventually require the enlightened minority's control over the benighted majority? As Mickelsson puts the question to his class: "Just how fascistic is Plato's *Republic*?" (94). Lawler's behavior—if we take it as the working out of an intellectual position rather than as a madman's whim—seems to answer Mickelsson's question. It exposes the dangers of an inflexible defense of absolute truth, which can become obsessive and which can even, in extreme instances, lead to violence. Mickelsson's own approach—"open-mindedness, subjecting one's opinions and prejudices to analysis and rigorous argument" (101)— seems preferable, although we have seen the anguishing internal dialogue to which it can lead. Seen in contrast to its opposite,

Mickelsson's intellectual confusion seems more honest and less dangerous.

Mickelsson's confrontation with Lawler brings a resolution of his spiritual crisis. He knows that Lawler will kill him once they have completed their fruitless search of the farmhouse. Driven by these desperate circumstances, he goes against all his rational training and begins to pray. He sends out a "mental cry" (550) both to the God in whom he has refused to believe and to the human community upon whom he has turned his back. In these intense minutes he will hear many of the voices of his cacophonous internal dialogues—his wife, his lawyer, Nietzsche, and Wittgenstein—and, temporarily at least, he will triumph over them. His desperate prayer will drown out Lawler's cynical commentary and his own lingering doubts. His voice will then join other voices—the legitimate cries for help of his daughter, his lover, and his colleagues—that heretofore he has refused to hear. Their blended cries will eventually bring rescue by a psychic child and her father. In his moment of extreme need, Mickelsson reaches out to God and to his fellow humans and is saved.

We note in this confrontation another juxtaposition of the child and the fat man. The child—in Mickelsson's Wisconsin memories, in Donnie's fetus, and in the Sprague dream—has represented innocence lost or murdered. The fat man has represented the bank robber's greed, Luther and Mickelsson's lust—enemies of the innocent child. The fat man reappears here in the corpulent Lawler, whom Mickelsson earlier has mistaken for the bank robber. Confronted by this fat man, embodying intellectual arrogance and cynicism, Mickelsson momentarily recovers the child's innocent faith in God and in his fellowman. The child in this scene—the innocent young psychic who hears his cry—now rescues Mickelsson.

Mickelsson's Return

Lawler has forced Mickelsson to dismantle the farmhouse that was the foundation of his independent existence. Mickelsson is now ready to return, for like James Chandler, he has learned that he cannot work out his salvation in isolation from others. In the novel's final scene Mickelsson returns to Binghamton for a faculty party where he confesses to Jessica, proposes marriage, and makes love to her; his reintegration into the community seems to have begun. Solutions to many of Mickelsson's problems arrive with astonishing celerity in the final pages. Donnie Mathews calls to announce her abortion and her becoming a born-again Christian. After the Lawler episode, the police refuse to prosecute Mickelsson for his crimes of theft and manslaughter, despite their sure knowledge of his guilt. His neighbors unite to clean up the damage inflicted by Lawler and to dig Mickelsson an uncontaminated well. Mickelsson is reconciled with his daughter, and, as a final bonus, his son, who had disappeared into the political underground, shows up on his couch. So sudden, and so poorly motivated, is this good fortune that it leaves us as unsatisfied and unconvinced as does the Lawler solution to the mystery.

And what of Mickelsson himself? We are heartened by his return to the human community, but nagging problems remain. Financially, he will have to make heavy alimony payments while trying to pay off his tax obligation and the many debts incurred in restoring his farmhouse. Perhaps Jessica, if she marries him, can introduce some economic order to his life. Psychologically, he initially believes that he is free of his ghosts. He soon discovers, however, that the Spragues are still in the farmhouse and that Luther, Nietzsche, and his psychiatrist are still in his thoughts. In fact, at the party he acquires a whole new set of ghosts, including Jessica's deceased husband, a crowd of humans and animals who watch his lovemaking with Jessica, and a mysterious fall of bones from the sky. Has Mickelsson finally passed from simple clairvoyance to madness?

Morally, his situation seems equally parlous. Earlier the same day he has decided to remain in the mountains and ask nothing of the universe, but now he is in town insisting that Jessica have sex with him immediately. This seem an odd form of resignation. It is also a strange form of social reintegration. He leads Jessica away, closes the door on their friends as, once again, he demands immediate satisfaction of his anarchic sexual desires. And what of the strange costume he has devised for himself: a moth-eaten hunting coat, striped formal pants, an Irish hunting cap, and make-up of ink and plaster dust? Earlier he has attacked the self-indulgent buffoonery of Luther and Nietzsche, but here he seems to have adopted it for himself. We began our discussion by comparing Mickelsson to James Chandler, but the figures we see profiled behind our protagonist in this final scene are those of the philosopher-buffoons: Agathon and Tag Hodge. We know too well the roots of such behavior—egoism and a deep despair—and its destructive consequences for us to be cheered by its appearance here.

Michael Nugent, Mickelsson's student, provides a commentary on the clown that can be applied to all of Gardner's buffoons:

You know how it is in the circus. The acrobat does something, and the clown tries to imitate it, but the clown's not human, like the acrobat, he's just this creature with straw in his head. That's why clowns are at the same time funny and sad: they imitate exactly what human beings do. . . . But no matter what they do they remain just clowns. . . . I just mean that you have to *believe* things, to be human—you know? You have to feel that things are *true*. A clown is someone who'd give his soul to believe, if he had one, but he never can, he just goes through the motions, harder and harder. (223–24)

As we watch Mickelsson lead Jessica to the coat-strewn bed and embrace her, we must ask ourselves whether he has finally found something in which he believes and in which he will continue to believe. Jessica, for her part, is not sure, and she worries that this all may simply be another of Mickelsson's "*fake* episodes" (589). If we share her doubts, if we are not certain that Mickelsson has discovered something he can continue to defend as *true*, can we be sure that he has finally recovered his humanity, that he is not simply a straw-headed clown? The conclusion of the last novel Gardner published before his death is, for me, profoundly ambiguous.

Chapter Eleven
Stillness and Shadows

In 1986, Nicholas Delbanco, Gardner's friend and literary executor, brought out two novelistic texts that Gardner had left unpublished at his death. Neither is finished and neither can stand with Gardner's best fictions, but, taken together, they serve as an appropriate coda to his career. Here we find, once again, many of the familiar problems and situations that we have followed through the earlier works. These narratives, in their respective strengths and weaknesses, also help us to better see the distinctive features of Gardner's fictional achievement.

Stillness and Moral Rebirth

Stillness (1986), the more finished of these pieces, resulted from Gardner and his first wife's attempt to save their foundering marriage. The novel portrays Martin and Joan Orrick, a novelist and a concert musician, whose marriage is filled with nearly murderous anger, resentment, and jealousy. The problem that this narrative sets for itself is the problem that Gardner introduced in his first published novel: the problem of moral rebirth. Can these two individuals take charge of their lives and change the behavior that is driving them apart? Can they save their marriage and—very possibly—their lives?

Although the Orricks fell in love as children and have spent nearly half of their lives married to each other, they are, in fact, strikingly different people. Martin is reason, industry, and intellectual order. We see him long hours at his desk, his stomach soured by too many cups of coffee, laboriously polishing his manuscript. Joan is intuition, flashing wit, the quick penetrating insight. She commands the attention of her dinner guests with her devastating impersonations and her rapier sharp put-downs. Martin mistrusts her raillery—he finds it facile and ungenerous—and tries to tie her to logic in their personal disputes. Joan resents his pomposity and bridles at the graduate-school erudition he marshalls in their arguments. She wishes he could set aside his specious rationalism and project himself intuitively into her situation and understand her suffering from inside. The contrast between them—left brain versus right brain, as Martin characterizes it—is great, and yet the divisions that lie within Martin and Joan individually are, in many ways, even greater. It becomes increasingly clear that they will be able to achieve domestic peace only if they can first lay to rest their personal, internal demons.

The problem that besets Martin is the same one that haunts other Gardnerian protagonists: the tension between chaos and order. Martin illustrates his problem for us dramatically when we watch him mesmerized by a gathering cyclone: exulting in its destructive power, he ducks into his storm shelter only at the last possible minute. The cyclone seems to embody his intuition of the ultimate violent and chaotic reality. He thrusts himself into the heart of this destructive disorder to better savor "the sweet stillness" that follows the storm's passing. He hopes to discover in that stillness an order, a sense that "everything in the universe was secretly connected."[1]

His bulwark against chaos is his art. He defines this art when he recalls how, as a boy, he would ascend the hill behind the family farm and play his French horn: "there, in sight of his neighbors' lights but as safely remote from their judgments and opinions as from the stars overhead, he would play his emotions without daring to name them. . . . He became in those moments, as he would become in his writing long afterward, a sort of human conduit, a spokesman for the ordinary human feelings coming up from the scattered lights below (and from his own chest) and a spokesman for the ice-cold absolutes in the black sky above him" (91). The artist's posture alone against the sky, surrounded by the dark forest—reminds us of the Thor whom Gardner evokes at the outset of *On Moral Fiction*. But the figure here is clearly human, no demigod, and the tone is different: the heroic confidence is absent and, with it, all troll-killing belligerence. This artist is uncertain "what it was—if anything at all—that his music was expressing" (91). The same is true, we are told, for the adult novelist: "Martin Orrick . . . would have no more idea what his novels meant than did the shelves on which they stood" (91). A different comparison, more apposite in this context than Thor, is with another young horn player, Terence Parks of *October Light*. That young musician, we remember, committed himself to pure music that had no greater ambition than to be, as honestly as possible, its simple note-by-note self. For Martin, as for Terence, there can be no self-conscious straining after significance; there can only be the "old-fashioned carpenter's stubborn, unambitious concern for workmanship" (91). Meaning, if there is any, only reveals itself later, adventitiously.

Art has an important function in the struggle against chaos, but the "sudden stillness" (62) it imposes is purely formal: the exhilarating, but finally meaningless flourishes of the skilled tap dancer. The fundamentally chaotic nature of reality—"the universal banging of atom against atom, planet against planet, heart against heart" (12)—remains unchanged. Martin recognizes but cannot quite accept this state of affairs; he wants desperately for life to imitate art, for a man's life to "develop reasonably, like a plot, with choices along the way, and antagonists with names, and some grand, compelling purpose, and a ringing final line" (74). But this desire for order is frustrated, not only on the cosmic level, but on the level of Martin's personal life as well. He continually ranges between periods of ascetic withdrawal and bouts of alcoholic and sexual excess, driving his wife further away with each dramatic cycle.

Joan Orrick's soul is as painfully divided as that of her husband. In her case the division results from the conflict of expectations and real achievements. Joan Frazier, as a child, struck all who knew her as truly remarkably for her beauty, her wit, and, especially, her music talent. She quickly outdistanced her local music tutor and was sent off to a distinguished teacher in St. Louis; her precocity was rewarded by a radio show and important concerts. And yet the adult Joan has never quite realized the potential promised by these beginnings. She married her cousin, subordinated her career to his, and began to suffer excruciating but inexplicable attacks of pain. Joan's suffering, it is finally determined, has definite physiological causes, and it also seems mysteriously related to her feelings for Martin. Her first attack occurs the night when, as a teenager, Martin first kissed her; and other attacks will follow the most dramatic and acrimonious fights with her husband. It is only after Joan decides to change the behavior that is destroying their marriage that she is able to use autohypnosis to control her pain.

The resolution of the Orrick conflict, as it exists in the uncompleted manuscript, is the least satisfactory element in this narrative. It is Joan who finally decides that "people can change, save themselves" (157), and who sets about to rescue their marriage. She visits Martin's mistress to learn how she might better please her husband. The astonished lover offers no advice, but she does withdraw her claims to Martin.

Joan then visits a psychiatrist who helps her eliminate the behavior that irritates Martin. She returns from her doctor, enters their house, announces "I'm home," and the novel ends. The first problem with this resolution is the sexism implicit in the suggestion that, to save her marriage, Joan Orrick has only to learn how to please her husband. This resolution, moreover, lets the male off the hook far too easily. As in the final pages of *Mickelsson's Ghost,* the male protagonist is welcomed back by the long-suffering female with no significant effort on his part to reform his egoistic and destructive behavior. An additional problem with this ending is credibility. It is simply too quick, too easy, and too one-sided to provide a believable solution to this complex conflict. The external breach may momentarily be healed, but the internal cleavages within Martin and Joan remain.

Structure and Point of View in *Stillness*

Although Gardner never completed *Stillness* to his satisfaction, he does seem to have found a structure suited to presenting the conflicts between and within Martin and Joan Orrick. The prologue establishes what will be the narrative present for most of the novel. The Orricks are in their forties and are living in the Missouri Ozarks where Martin teaches in a newly created university. Their marriage has reached a dangerous crisis point. From this moment the novel will move back over the period before their coming to Missouri (chapters 1 to 13), then through that period (chapters 14 to 18), and finally beyond that period to their new life in Bennington, Vermont (chapter 19). The three-part structure thus corresponds roughly to their crisis, the events leading to it, and their attempt to move past it.

The first thing to notice about this structure is the importance of the past—over 60 percent of the book is devoted to events prior to the novel's opening. We are also struck by the fact that half of that space—roughly a third of the total narrative—is devoted to histories of the Orrick's ancestors, parents, and friends. But these portions are crucial, for both Martin and Joan are obsessed by the past. Martin, blessed—or perhaps cursed—with a nearly photographic memory, is haunted by recollections of what he has seen and heard of the older members of their family. These ancestors represent, for Martin, a nearly Homeric Golden Age: men "such as men were then and are not now" (34). Like Peter Mickelsson, he feels a profound nostalgia for their sturdy religious faith. John Frazier, Joan's grandfather and Martin's grandmother's brother, is an instance: this practicing Baptist actively embodied the Gospel message, befriending blacks when they were still persecuted in Missouri. For Joan, her recollections are of the achievements of her artistic mentors, the initial promise of her own career, and the frustrated expectations of her family.

Rather than a solace, these memories are a bitter wound for Martin and Joan, because they embody an implicit reproach to the religious and moral indifference into which they have fallen and from which they seem unable to escape. One memory is a particularly ironic contrast to their present condition. Martin recalls Sunday dinners at his grandfather's house. Seated at a table laden with the fruits of the farm, the family would review the morning's sermon and then launch into a spirited but civil discussion of religion, politics, and literature. The memories of these meals—suggesting a secure faith, solid marriages, and generous tolerance to other points of view—compare harshly with the scenes around the Orrick's dinner table, where Martin's tedious pontifications might be interrupted by Joan's angry profanity or even by physical assault.

The setting of the novel's central portion, already introduced in the prologue, is crucial. When his marriage goes bad in San Francisco, Martin chooses to accept a position at a new univesity in the Missouri Ozarks. He is motivated, in part, by love for the area where he spent his boyhood summers, an area he associates with his and Joan's ancestors. He is thus imitating Peter Mickelsson who sought to recover his Wisconsin boyhood in the Pennsylvania hills. But there is also an uglier side to Martin's choice. He knows that Joan hates Missouri and that the move will cut her off even further from her musical career, and yet he seems, perversely, to wish to put her commitment to him to the test. Finally, as we have seen in his fascination with the cyclone, there is something dramatic and violent in this flood and storm threatened land that corresponds to Martin's intuition of the ultimate, chaotic reality. The days in this landscape are the most tumultuous of their marriage, filled with drunken, nearly suicidal horseback rides by Martin and angry, despairing recriminations by Joan.

Fortunately, the move to Missouri also introduces them to the Ferndeans. This lively, happily married couple, a British sculptor and his wife, seem to inspire the Orricks with the hope that their marriage too might once again be happy. When John Ferndean dies of cancer they are, of course, deeply saddened, and yet some of his spirit seems to have entered into them. Not long after Ferndean's passing, the Orricks decide to leave Missouri for New England and, aided by friends, set about to try to save their marriage. The idyllic Vermont village gives them new energy, and Joan sets about to make the changes we have described. Still, Martin is likely to need his extramarital affairs, and Joan will probably rebel against them. The future, as always with Gardner, remains open.

One final technical element, point of view, requires comment, since it significantly effects the novel's meaning. The novel is focused through a narrator who limits himself, for the most part, to what the characters themselves know. Occasionally, however, he will give us information that the characters did not know at the precise moment being narrated but that they will realize later. By enlarging the perspective slightly in this fashion he is able to present more reflective and mature judgments. The narrator focuses roughly half of the chapters through Martin's point of view and roughly half through Joan's, with one chapter presented through Joan's mother's point of view. As a consequence, the narrative embodies that "childlike fairness" (168) attributed to Martin's novels, and we have the sense of a balanced, even-handed presentation of the Orrick's problems.

Stillness, as we have it, more closely resembles in size, structure, and tone Gardner's *Resurrection* and *Nickel Mountain* than it does works like *The Sunlight Dialogues* or *Mickelsson's Ghosts.* As with *Nickel Mountain,* the novel is a collection of closely related stories. Gardner, in fact, published two portions of this novel, only slightly changed, as the stories "Stillness" and "Redemption" in *The Art of Living.* Here, as in the histories of Henry and Callie Soames, the emphasis is much more on the observation of individual behavior than on the exploration of large philosophic schemes. Both works place primary emphasis on recounting the characters' experiences, allowing the deeper resonances to emerge on their own rather than from excessive, self-conscious intellectual commentary.

The material in *Stillness* was, for Gardner, achingly personal, so it is very likely that he would never have completed it. Nicholas Delbanco has, however, given us an idea of the shape it might have taken had he chosen to go on with it: "His characteristic method . . . had to do with expansion: filling in the blanks. He planned to do so here. He spoke of his intention, how the 'stillness' at the novel's center would connect to problems of particle physics, to tornadoes in the Ozarks, to Japanese theater—the Sarugakah No Noh. . . . Such matters are but adumbrated in this draft. The pages are open, a few corrections penciled in; he ended where the thickening would otherwise begin" (xiii). These plans, to me, do not seem promising, and I cannot regret Gardner's failure to follow through on them. The Orrick's story, although incomplete, is moving and significant on its own; it hardly seems to require "thickening" doses of molecular physics, meterology, or Japanese drama.

Multiple Shadows in *Shadows*

Shadows (1986) is a much more ambitious and much less complete work. The central problems with which it meant to deal are, however, fairly clear, and they will be familiar to readers of Gardner's other fictions. The protagonist, a detective named Craine, who is in pursuit of a serial murderer, moves in a world of shadows. The novel's title refers, in the first instance, to the shadow of death, for Craine has recently survived cancer surgery, but he has no guarantee that the disease will not recur. He thus lives in the same twilight zone inhabited by James Chandler. But the novel's title is plural, and there are other shades with which Craine must deal. Ira Katz, Craine's fellow resident in a seedy hotel, explains the obscurities created in our lives by failed ideals:

We have an idea of ourselves, when we're kids: noble-hearted, honorable, unselfish. It's a beautiful image, and in fact it's true—it's the truth about us—but we betray it, or the nature of the world betrays it. . . . We can't do what's decent. Our commitments prevent it, or it's beyond our means. There are only so many causes you can die for, only so many good women you can love with all your heart. . . . So we lose touch with ourselves, turn our backs on the image. . . . The image is still there, the shadow we cast into the future when we were young. It's still there haunting us, beckoning us toward it; only now there is that second shadow, the shadow, behind us, of all those acts unworthy of us. (268–69)

Craine, like Peter Mickelsson and Martin Orrick, is the descendant of devout Christians from whom he has inherited a sense of life's lofty possibilities. Like these two and like Agathon, Craine has had to deal with the disappointment of his expectations. His particular strategy has been to deny the past, shut off all memories, and live in a perpetual present. The ruse does not quite work, and, as the narrative progresses, his consciousness is penetrated by vivid and painful recollections of the past.

The novel's epigraph suggests another meaning of the novel's title and introduces the ontological and epistemological questions that have troubled many of Gardner's characters: "The external world of physics," Sir Arthur Eddington writes, "has become a world of shadows. In removing our illusion we have removed the substance, for indeed we have seen that substance is one of the greatest of our illusions." The epigraph questions the ultimate nature of reality and the possibility of ever knowing it. Craine, like Grendel, has grave doubts on this point (176). These doubts carry serious consequences for a private detective. His function, in the detective genre's parlance, is to be a "shadow"— an obscurity who casts light: his role is to follow, to observe, and, ultimately, to resolve questions of identity and guilt.

Craine and Ira Katz discuss the detective's function in a conversation that Gardner must have intended as central to the novel's dialogue. For Craine, ultimate reality is unknowable, and so the best that a detective can do is to make up a theory and stake his life on it. To do so, he must remain dispassionate, outside time—"a man with no earthly connections, suspicious as a rat" (257). Katz sees things differently. He holds out the possibility of a truth that would correspond to what God sees. He urges the detective to tease out the rules that control our behavior, "to figure out what the secret laws are for sentient mammals—what hurts us and what doesn't, physically, psychologically, spiritually. . . . We should work at discovering what values are built into us. Learn to survive—learn what makes us *fit*" (261). Katz, a Christ-like poet, opposes the detective's cold-eyed withdrawal and favors passionate engagement: "We have only two ways of finding out what's true, what will work. By history's blind groping, one damn thing after another, as they say . . . or by rigorous imagination, which in the end means by poems and novels" (262–63). Craine, perhaps, is tempted, but in the novelistic fragments Gardner left us he remains unconvinced. Had Gardner continued, he almost certainly would have attempted to work out and test these opposed positions.

Just how successful that working out might have been is far from clear. The portions Gardner left us seem to consist largely of the "thickening"—windy disquisitions on a variety of subjects—that he apparently felt *Stillness* lacked. In the first chapter Craine learns he is being followed and discusses with a medical professor the connection of the

mind and the "bioplasmic universe"; in chapter 2 he is questioned
about a series of murders and holds forth on Sanscrit theories of language; a little later he is hired by his mysterious pursuer and uses the
occasion to discuss the archaeology of matriarchal societies. In the two
hundred plus pages that he left us, Gardner tells us about complementarity in physics, theories of time, and the effect of computers on our
idea of reality, but he has not advanced his detective story much beyond
the basic elements I have listed. The murder story, as Dostoyevski,
Faulkner, and Borges have shown, can be the means for exploring serious and intellectually challenging themes. But detective fiction,
perhaps more than any other genre, demands a solid narrative architecture. This, we remember, was the signal weakness of *Mickelsson's
Ghosts,* Gardner's earlier attempt to use the mystery form, and it is
again an important weakness in this text. Rather than build a narrative, Gardner seems more interested here in propping his characters up
in a doorframe and allowing them to expatiate on psychology, science,
and metaphysics.

Stillness and Shadows are very different works. The former emphasizes
narrative and the closely observed description of character; its tone is
restrained and realistic. The latter gives priority to the discussion of
large philosophical questions; its tone is often cartoonish, creating
larger-than-life grotesques. The publication of these two texts in the
same volume reminds us of the variety of elements to be found in
Gardner's fiction. This variety illustrates an important point made by
historians and theoreticians of the novel. Mikhail Bakhtin, Northrop
Frye, Robert Scholes, and Robert Kellogg agree in seeing the novel
not as a pure form, but as a hybrid. The novel grows out of, develops,
and combines forms as disparate as the epic, the romance, the confession, the pastoral, the moral fable, and the philosophical dialogue.
This hybrid nature is, for Bakhtin, a source of its power as a dialogical
form, a genre dedicated to bringing heterogeneous elements into fruit-
ful and illuminating conjunction. This conjoining can only become
truly dialogical—that is, not merely present issues but bring them into
conflict and test them—when it is built on the element that Aristotle
regarded as the soul of all narrative: a clear, solidly constructed plot.

All of the forms I have listed, and more, can be found in Gardner's
fictions, often in combination. Some of his fictions—*Stillness,* for instance—seem more realistic and pyschological; others—like *Sunlight
Dialogues* and *Mickelsson's Ghosts*—emphasize ideas; but all are hybrids.

For me, the most successful of his works—I would list *Nickel Mountain, Grendel,* and *October Light*—are the ones that have a clear central narrative—the development of one or more characters. The intellectual content is complex and significant, but it is part of the meat and sinew of the characters rather than flabby padding.

Gardner's Achievement: A Universe of Voices

In John Gardner's fictional world all meanings seem ambiguous. Gardner, who began his university studies as a chemistry student, frequently turns to science to help explain this state of affairs. We have already mentioned his use, as an epigraph, of Sir Arthur Eddington's comments on the way modern physics has dissolved the seemingly solid world of physical substance. Later in *Shadows* Gardner has a character draw out the implications of the modern physicist's view of the world. It is less, it turns out, a situation in which we can never know reality or discover meaning than it is one in which those meanings will always be multiple. Here is that character's explanation of complementarity in physics:

The physical universe may be constructed in completely different ways, so that it shows itself to us in one way or another depending on how we look at it. Ask questions that assume light travels in waves, and the universe obliges us by answering in waves. Ask questions that assume that light flows in particles, and the universe answers you in particles. There's no resolving the conflict—no "wavicles," as some scientific wag once expressed it. The universe is this, but also that—that's complementarity. (196–97)

In discussing the problem of meaning, Gardner's characters also frequently have recourse to biology and evolution. *Grendel*'s dragon is an instance. He tells us that reality is not only shadowy but dynamic as well; the shadows we see today are not the same we saw yesterday. The implication for this cynical monster—as for Agathon, Grendel, and Tag Hodge—is that the entire search for understanding is absurd.

But there are other voices less discouraging. Lane Walker reminds *October Light*'s disputants of the way reality is constantly changing and warns them of generalizing too quickly based on the past or on their expectations of the future. He does not, however, give up on the effort to understand, and there are other important voices in Gardner's fictional world who agree. This point is worth making to call attention to the fact that, although Gardner is fully alive to the ambiguity that is central to much postmodernist writing, his world still offers the hope of meaning, although the meanings may be multiple, conflicting, and transitory. The phrase that occurs several times in his novels—"the buzzing blooming confusion"[2] of life—suggests not despair but affectionate acceptance of our chaotic, confounding world. The characters who live most successfully in this world—the individuals whose behavior the narratives test and confirm—are those like Peeker, Henry Soames, Fred Clumly, and Lars-Goren Berquist who accept and even embrace life's fundamental ambiguity. These individuals—Gardner's "heroes"—embody a generous and tolerant openness of heart and mind.

This ethic of openness has aesthetic implications, and these are, I believe, embodied in the structure of Gardner's narratives. In all but two of these, the narration is focused through several, or many, quite different point-of-view characters. In those two instances where the narrative is focused through a single character—in *Grendel* and in *Mickelsson's Ghosts*—these characters are themselves caught in contentious internal dialogues. Thus we are forced to consider the issues raised in the narrative from several quite different angles. In addition, these narratives are themselves multiple. The problems confronted by James Chandler, Henry Soames, and Fred Clumly echo in the lives of the other characters with whom their own lives intersect. We have also noted in these narratives a reluctance to force the conflict to a neat resolution. We are typically left at the ends of these novels with an open situation that offers a number of possible interpretations. Finally, we have also seen in these novel's metafictional commentary a kind of act of authorial humility, an acknowledgment that what we have is an artist's subjective ordering of the world and not a piece of the world itself. We are invited into the dialogue and required to render our own judgment on the issues dramatized in the narrative.

I ended my introductory chapter with Gardner's description of the openness required of one who would write fiction. It was from a work published after his death. I would like to conclude with another posthumously published comment by Gardner, part of his introduction to *Shadows*. In it Gardner describes the open, dialogical form that he attempted in his narratives. It can stand as an appropriate summation of the fictional universe we have been exploring. "My ideal novel is a universe of voices, not a work of triumphant individual will but a human chorus, sometimes in harmony, sometimes not . . . a concatenation in which I, the novelist, serve mainly as moderator, keeping the various contributions more or less relevant both in the sense that they apply and in the sense that they tend to move the whole kaboodle in some direction that satisfies my intuition of where things ought to go" (361).

Notes and References

Preface

1. *Fiction International*, no. 12 (1980).

Chapter One

1. *On Moral Fiction* (New York: Basic Books, 1978), 18. Subsequent page references in the text.
2. Gerald Graff, *Literature against Itself* (Chicago: University of Chicago Press, 1979), 31–62.
3. John Barth, "The Literature of Replenishment," *Atlantic* 245 (January 1980):67.
4. Digby Diehl, "Book Talk: Medievalist in Illinois Ozarks," *Los Angeles Times*, 5 September 1971, 43.
5. Joe David Bellamy, *The New Fiction: Interviews with Innovative American Writers* (Urbana: University of Illinois Press, 1974), 182.
6. "I wrote that book [*On Moral Fiction*] in 1964. I had not yet been published. I was furious—just enraged at those guys with big reputations—and I wrote a vituperative, angry book." Curt Suplee, "John Gardner, Flat Out," *Washington Post*, 25 July 1982, p. H8.
7. Wayne Booth, *The Company We Keep: An Ethics of Fiction* (Berkeley: University of California Press, 1988), 70.
8. Ibid., 485.
9. Mikhail Bakhtin, *Problems of Dostoevsky's Poetics*, ed. and trans. Caryl Emerson (Minneapolis: University of Minnesota Press, 1984), 6.
10. *On Becoming a Novelist* (New York: Harper & Row, 1983), 32.

Chapter Two

1. *The Resurrection* (New York: Ballantine Books, 1974), 114. Subsequent page references in the text. Because Gardner made a number of changes from the hardcover text (New York: New American Library, 1966), I have chosen to use the paperback edition..
2. Marshall Harvey, "Where Philosophy and Fiction Meet: An Interview with John Gardner," *Chicago Review* 29 (Spring 1978):82. These comments should be set against Gardner's praise of Tolstoy in *On Moral Fiction* to remind us of the inconsistencies between that book and Gardner's statements and practice elsewhere.
3. L. N. Tolstoy, *Resurrection*, trans. Rosemary Edmonds (New York: Penguin Books, 1966), 19.

4. Bakhtin, *Problems*, 56.
5. Ibid., 68.

Chapter Three

1. *The Wreckage of Agathon* (New York: Harper & Row, 1970), 167. Subsequent page references in the text.
2. See Michael André Bernstein, "When the Carnival Turns Bitter," in *Bakhtin: Essays and Dialogues on His Works*, ed. Gary Saul Morson (Chicago: University of Chicago Press, 1981), 99–122.

Chapter Four

1. *Grendel* (New York: Alfred A. Knopf, 1971), 21–22. Subsequent page references in the text.
2. For some of these references see Michael Ackland, "Blakean Sources in John Gardner's *Grendel*," *Critique: Studies in Modern Fiction* 23 (1981):57–66; W. P. Fitzpatrick; "Down and Down I Go: A Note on Shelley's *Prometheus Unbound* and Gardner's *Grendel*," *Notes on Contemporary Literature* 7 (1977):2–5; Joseph Milosh, "John Gardner's *Grendel*: Sources and Analogues," *Contemporary Literature* 19 (1978):48–57; David Minugh, "John Gardner Constructs *Grendel*'s Universe," in *Studies in English Philology, Linguistics and Literature Presented to Alarik Rynell*, eds. Mats Ryden and Lennard A. Bjork (Stockholm: Almqvist & Wiksell, 1978), 125–41; Joseph F. Tuso, "*Grendel*, Chapter 1: John Gardner's Perverse Prologue," *College Literature* 12 (1985):184–86.
3. See Craig J. Stromme, "The Twelve Chapters of *Grendel*," *Critique: Studies in Modern Fiction* 20 (1978):83–93.

Chapter Five

1. Quoted in Heide Zeigler, "John Gardner," in *The Radical Imagination and the Liberal Tradition*, eds. Heide Ziegler and Chris Bigsby (London: Junction Books, 1982), 134.
2. Ibid., 134–35.
3. *The Sunlight Dialogues* (New York: Alfred A. Knopf, 1972), 407. Subsequent page references in the text.

Chapter Six

1. See Per Winther, "An Interview With John Gardner," *English Studies: A Journal of Language and Literature* 62 (1981):519.
2. *Jason and Medeia* (New York: Alfred A. Knopf, 1973), 82. Subsequent page references in the text. I have followed Gardner's transliteration of the Greek names.

Chapter Seven

1. *Nickel Mountain* (New York: Alfred A. Knopf, 1973), 148. Subsequent page references in the text.
2. Gérard Genette, *Narrative Discourse: An Essay in Method,* trans. Jane E. Lewin (Ithaca, N.Y.: Cornell University Press, 1980), 116.

Chapter Eight

1. *October Light* (New York: Alfred A. Knopf, 1976), 430. Subsequent page references in the text.
2. Gregory L. Morris, *A World of Order and Light: The Fiction of John Gardner* (Athens: University of Georgia Press, 1984), 156.
3. *The Art of Fiction: Notes on Craft for Young Writers* (New York: Vintage, 1985), 49.

Chapter Nine

1. *Freddy's Book* (New York: Alfred A. Knopf, 1980), 33. Subsequent page references in the text.

Chapter Ten

1. *Mickelsson's Ghosts* (New York: Alfred A. Knopf, 1982), 170. Subsequent page references in the text.

Chapter Eleven

1. *"Stillness" and "Shadows"* (New York: Alfred A. Knopf, 1986), 128. Subsequent page references in the text.
2. *The Resurrection,* 229; *Nickel Mountain,* 193; *Jason and Medeia,* 129.

Selected Bibliography

PRIMARY WORKS

Novels

Freddy's Book. New York: Alfred A. Knopf, 1980.
Grendel. New York: Alfred A. Knopf, 1971.
Mickelsson's Ghosts. New York: Alfred A. Knopf, 1982.
Nickel Mountain. New York: Alfred A. Knopf, 1973.
October Light. New York: Alfred A. Knopf, 1976.
The Resurrection. New York: Ballantine Books, 1974.
"Stillness" and "Shadows". New York: Alfred A. Knopf, 1986.
The Sunlight Dialogues. New York: Alfred A. Knopf, 1972.
The Wreckage of Agathon. New York: Harper & Row, 1970.

Narrative Poem

Jason and Medeia. New York: Alfred A. Knopf, 1973.

Story Collections

The Art of Living. New York: Alfred A. Knopf, 1981.
The King's Indian: Stories and Tales. New York: Alfred A. Knopf, 1974.

Critical and Scholarly Books

The Alliterative Morte Arthure. Carbondale: Southern Illinois University Press, 1971.
The Art of Fiction: Notes on Craft for Young Writers. New York: Vintage, 1985.
The Complete Works of the Gawain-Poet. Chicago: University of Chicago Press, 1965.
The Construction of Christian Poetry in Old English. Carbondale: Southern Illinois University Press, 1975.
The Construction of The Wakefield Cycle. Carbondale: Southern Illinois University Press, 1974.
The Life and Times of Chaucer. New York: Alfred A. Knopf, 1977.
On Becoming a Novelist. New York: Harper & Row, 1983.
On Moral Fiction. New York: Basic Books, 1978.
The Poetry of Chaucer. Carbondale: Southern Illinois University Press, 1977.

SECONDARY WORKS

Bibliographies

Howell, John M. *John Gardner: A Bibliographical Profile*. Carbondale: Southern Illinois University Press, 1980. A full listing through 1979 of Gardner's books, reviews, letters, interviews, etc. Updated to 1983 by Lee T. Hamilton, "John Gardner: A Bibliographical Update" in Mendez-Egle listed below.

Morace, Robert A. *John Gardner: An Annotated Secondary Bibliography*. New York: Garland Publishers, 1984. A full listing through 1983 of interviews with Gardner as well as reviews and criticism of his work. Includes generous and useful annotations.

Critical Studies and Collections of Critical Essays

Begiebing, Robert J. *Toward a New Synthesis: John Fowles, John Gardner, Norman Mailer*. Ann Arbor, Mich.: UMI Research Press, 1989. Studies Gardner, Fowles, and Mailer to show how each novelist transcends the distance between the world and art. Studies the ethical basis of experimentation and the magician figure in *The Sunlight Dialogues*.

Butts, Leonard. *The Novels of John Gardner: Making Life Art as Moral Process*. Baton Rouge: Louisiana State University Press, 1988. Focuses on the "moral artists" in the novels and studies the way the protagonists move toward a unifying vision or fail to break out of a limited vision of the world.

Cowart, David. *Arches and Light: The Fiction of John Gardner*. Carbondale: Southern Illinois University Press, 1983. Discusses how Gardner attempted in his fiction to build a solid foundation across the modern moral abyss. Includes analysis of Gardner's short fiction as well as the novels.

Henderson, Jeff, ed. *Thor's Hammer: Essays on John Gardner*. Conway, Ark.: University of Central Arkansas Press, 1985. Includes essays on Gardner's apprenticeship, Gardner as editor, as poet, and as translator, as well as essays on Gardner's literary theory and his fiction.

Mendez-Egle, Beatriz, ed. *John Gardner: True Art, Moral Art*. Living Authors Series, no. 5. Edinboro, Texas: Pan American University School of Humanities, 1983. Includes essays on *Jason and Medeia* as well as essays on the fiction, an update of the Howell bibliography, and an interview with Gardner.

Morace, Robert A., and Kathryn VanSpanckeren, eds. *John Gardner: Critical Perspectives*. Carbondale: Southern Illinois University Press, 1982. Includes essays on Gardner's novels, short fiction, children's fiction, libretti, and poetry as well as an afterword by Gardner.

Morris, Gregory L. *A World of Order and Light: The Fictions of John Gardner.* Athens: University of Georgia Press, 1984. Analyzes Gardner's effort to discover order in the world and to present that order in his fiction. Includes chapters on the novels, on "The Old Men," Gardner's Ph.D. dissertation novel, and on his short fiction.

Index

Apollonious of Rhodes, 53–55, 59
Aristotle, 120
Arnold, Matthew, 40
astrology, 41

Bakhtin, Mikhail, 7–9, 17, 18, 22, 29, 120
Babylonian civilization, 45
Barth, John, 3, 4, 5, 83
Barthelme, Donald, 4, 5
Bellow, Saul, 4
Beowulf, 38, 41
Blake, William, 40–41
Booth, Wayne, 6–7
Borges, Jorge Luis, 120
Buechner, Frederick, 4
buffoon figure, 22–24, 26, 110–11

carnival in Bakhtin and Gardner, 22
Chaucer, 2, 40, 60
Cheever, John, 4
Chia Yi, 60
complementarity in physics and fiction, 121
Coover, Robert, 4
Crews, Harry, 4

Dante, 2, 60
Delbanco, Nicholas, 112, 117
detective story form in Gardner's novels, 108, 119
dialogical form, 7–9, 17, 29, 33, 40, 42–43, 54, 55, 62–63, 74, 83, 85–87, 89, 95, 101, 120, 122–23
Diehl, Digby, 5
Doctorow, E. L., 4
Dostoevsky, Fyodor, 17, 19

Eddington, Sir Arthur, 119, 121
Elkin, Stanley, 4, 5
Ellison, Ralph, 5
epic, 7–8, 38–40, 53–54, 61
Epictetus, 11

Euripides, 53–54, 59
existentialism, 25, 30

Faulkner, William, 120
Francis, Saint, 11
Frye, Northrup, 120

Gardner, John
    WORKS—CRITICAL BOOKS
    Art of Fiction, The, 85
    On Becoming a Novelist, 9
    On Moral Fiction, 1–9, 113

    WORKS—NOVELS
    Freddy's Book, 88–100, 122
    Grendel, 29–41, 42, 53–54, 61, 77, 98, 119, 121, 122
    Jason and Medeia, 53–61
    Mickelsson's Ghosts, 101–11, 116, 117, 118, 120, 122
    Nickel Mountain, 62–73, 117, 121, 122
    October Light, 74–87, 113, 121
    Resurrection, The, 10–19, 20, 21, 51, 62, 63, 101, 109, 122
    Shadows, 118–23
    Stillness, 112–18
    Sunlight Dialogues, The, 42–52, 62, 110, 117, 120, 121, 122
    Wreckage of Agathon, The, 20–28, 46, 62, 102, 110, 118, 121, 122

    WORKS—SHORT STORIES
    "Redemption," 117
    "Stillness," 117

Gass, William, 3, 4, 5
Genette, Gérard, 66
Gide, André, 12
Gilgamesh, 61
Graff, Gerald, 3

Heidegger, Martin, 12
Heller, Joseph, 4

Hitler, Adolf, 11
Homer, 2, 55, 115

iterative mode of narration, 66

Kant, Immanuel, 114, 117
Kellog, Robert, 120
Kinsella, Thomas, 40

Luther, Martin, 105–106, 109, 110

Mailer, Norman, 4
Malamud, Bernard, 4
Marx, Karl, 11
Medeia (Euripides), 53
"Mental Traveller, The" (William
    Blake), 40
metafiction and Gardner's novels, 38,
    54, 74, 83–87
Milton, John, 40
morality in art, 2–7, 16–17, 56–57,
    84–87
Mormonism, 107–108

Nietzsche, Friedrick, 106, 109, 110
Notke, Bernt, 94

pastoral, 62
Percy, Walker, 4

Porter, Katherine Ann, 4
postmodernism, 3, 122
Pynchon, Thomas, 3, 122

Republic, The (Plato), 108
Resurrection (Leo Tolstoy), 17
romantic artist, 3

Sartre, Jean-Paul, 25
Scholes, Robert, 120
Schopenhauer, Arthur, 60
Shakespeare, William, 60
Shelley, Percy Bysshe, 40
"Sonata for Four Horns" (Sir Michael
    Tippett), 86

time, experiences in, 65–68
Tolstoy, Leo, 2, 17–20
Tractatus (Ludwig Wittgenstein), 106
tragedy, 61
Tyler, Anne, 4

Updike, John, 4

Vonnegut, John, 40
Voyage of the Argonauts (Apollonious of
    Rhodes), 53

Wittgenstein, Ludwig, 106, 109